The Uncertain Future of the Lower Fraser

by
Anthony H. J. Dorcey
Irving K. Fox
Kenneth J. Hall
Thomas G. Northcote
Kenneth G. Peterson
Mark H. Sproule-Jones
John H. Weins

Edited by Anthony H.J. Dorcey

Westwater Research Centre
University of British Columbia

Distributed by
University of British Columbia Press

Westwater Research Centre
University of British Columbia
Vancouver, B.C. V6T 1W5

Westwater Research Centre was established in 1971. Its function is to conduct interdisciplinary research on problems concerning water resources and their associated lands. The Centre aims to provide an informed foundation for decisions about policies and institutional arrangements through rigorous analysis of the alternative courses of action that might be undertaken. The Centre publishes its results in books, a periodical bulletin, *Westwater,* and a series of technical reports.

Back cover photograph: Alevins, courtesy of Fisheries and Marine Service, D.O.E.

"Based on a series of seven lectures given . . . in Vancouver between January and March, 1976."

Includes index.
ISBN 0-920146-00-7

1. Water — Pollution — Fraser River, B.C. — Addresses, essays, lectures. 2. Water quality — British Columbia — Fraser River — Addresses, essays, lectures. I. Dorcey, Anthony H.J. II. Westwater Research Centre.

TD227.B7U53   628.1'68'0971133
                     C76-016042-2

PREFACE

When the Westwater Research Centre got underway during the summer of 1971 the initial issue it faced was what kind of investigation should the new Centre launch as its first major project. After reviewing various possibilities in a series of seminars with interested members of the general public, government officials, students and university faculty members it was decided that our first major investigation would be concerned with the control of pollution in the Lower Fraser — that portion of the Fraser River drainage below Hope. In the spring of 1972 our study was launched and in March of 1976 after nearly four years investigation the project was concluded. During the months of January, February and March 1976 the Westwater staff presented a series of seven lectures in the auditorium of the H.R. MacMillan Planetarium in Vancouver in which it summarized its findings and conclusions. This volume is based on those lectures.

The purpose of the lectures was to report to the general public in non-technical language what was learned in the course of the research investigations. Although about 30 technical reports on this research will be published, it was concluded that inasmuch as the research was conducted with public funds and since pollution is a matter of general public concern, the Centre had a responsibility to report its findings in a manner that would make them readily available to everyone who is interested in the control of pollution of the Lower Fraser. This volume is based on the same premise. We hope that it summarizes our findings in a form that makes them easily understood by anyone interested in the future of the Lower Fraser. An understanding of the coverage and major findings of the study can be obtained quickly by reading the Summary and Conclusions at the end of each chapter.

At the end of each chapter the technical studies on which the chapter is based are cited. While some of these were not yet published when this volume went to press, those interested in the technical reports can arrange to be notified when each report becomes available by contacting the Centre.

In offering this report we recognize and appreciate that many things have been done and are continuing to be done to improve water quality in the Lower Fraser system. Many people in public agencies and private organizations have been and are continuing to contribute to these advances and we know that Westwater's contribution has been a modest one. The special contribution — if any — that we have made stems from our effort to examine water pollution control in a comprehensive fashion including the relationships among the aquatic eco-system, waste discharges and the institutions for exercising control of pollution.

We wish to thank the many individuals who have cooperated and assisted us in so many ways in carrying out the programme of research on the Lower Fraser we have conducted over the past four years. These have included colleagues at the three universities, many students, agency personnel from all three levels of government, and numerous private individuals. We are grateful to the Inland Waters Directorate and the Fisheries and Marine Service of Environment

Canada, to the Canada Council and to the University of British Columbia for providing the funds which have supported this research. It is difficult to express how deeply we have appreciated the opportunity we have been afforded to serve the public in dealing with this important environmental problem.

It is only fitting to conclude this preface with an expression of my deep personal appreciation to those who have made a special contribution to this effort:

— To the authors who have worked so hard and faithfully on the research, the lectures, and the writing of this volume.
— To Anthony Dorcey for his conscientious devotion to editing and guiding the production of this book.
— To the numerous faculty members and students of B.C. universities who have contributed to the research on the Lower Fraser.
— To Jerry Pladsen, Darlene Nickull and Joyce Babula for typing, retyping and then retyping again the drafts of the lectures and the chapters.
— To Phyllis Rickman for accurately maintaining our accounts so that budgets were not exceeded.
— To Itsuo Yesaki both for his analytical work and the preparation of the charts and figures.
— To Fitch Cady for helping us in so many ways in making both the lectures and this volume understandable.
— To Lillian Mack for preparing the index, and last but not least
— to my wife, Rosemary, for her editorial assistance, including the translation of our crude prose into acceptable English!

Irving K. Fox

June, 1976   Director

CONTENTS

Preface
Irving K. Fox

1

Introduction

A pollution control programme has many facets ranging from the acquisition of knowledge of the effects of pollutants upon human health and aquatic ecosystems to the development of legal and administrative arrangements for regulating the discharge of wastes to a river system. Westwater's research project on pollution control for the Lower Fraser River has sought to embrace these several facets of the problem rather than being limited to one or two particular aspects. The investigation which it undertook addressed the following specific questions:

1. *What is the current condition of the Lower Fraser and its tributaries and what is its future outlook?* Stated another way, an effort was made to determine what pollutants are found in the river, how serious a problem they cause, and what the prospects are for either further degradation or enhancement of the water environment.

2. *What are the sources of pollution?* To control pollution effectively one must know where it comes from. Thus, an effort was made to arrive at a better understanding of activities which contribute pollutants to the Lower Fraser system.

3. *What technical means are available for reducing the discharge of pollutants to the river system?* While some types of wastes can be rendered harmless by processing in a treatment plant, it is well recognized that conventional treatment does not remove all pollutants and that in some cases waste discharge can be reduced more efficiently through a change in industrial processes or reclamation of waste materials. In addition some pollutants flow directly to the river system without entering sewers that lead to treatment plants. The study examined a range of technologies that might be utilized to reduce pollution discharges to the Lower Fraser.

4. *How can waste producers be best induced to limit their waste discharges to appropriate levels?* Law, regulations, subsidies, and taxes have been utilized to induce waste producers to limit their waste discharges. Whichever method or combination of methods is used, the regulatory body requires information about who the waste producers are and how much they are discharging. The research project sought to generate information which would aid in understanding the kinds of policy mechanisms best suited to the Lower Fraser.

5. *What framework of law and what distribution of responsibilities among public agencies are required to carry-out an effective programme of pollution control in the Lower Fraser?* The control of pollution requires one or more public agencies to implement the policies and programmes decided upon. These agencies must function under authority established in law. An important objective of the project was to assess the existing legal-administrative framework and determine what steps, if any could be taken to strengthen this framework.

Needless to say it was not practicable with the resources available to the Centre to provide full and complete answers to these five questions. Considering the size of the area and the complexity of the problems addressed, the funding available to the Centre — about $600,000 for the total study — was modest. However, even if a much larger investment were made, full and complete answers are unlikely to be found for two reasons. One is that both the physical-biological aspects of pollution and the decision processes of a society — its legal and administrative procedures — are so intricate that an enormous investment would be required to provide an accurate and comprehensive picture of the problem at a given moment in time. The other is that pollution problems are in a continuous state of change because new products are being developed each year (and some of these are destined to become pollutants), water use and associated land uses do not remain the same, and social preferences (or values) keep evolving. Therefore the Westwater staff does not presume to have final solutions to pollution problems of the Lower Fraser. It is our hope, however, that the Centre's work will enable the problems to be defined more precisely, that it will suggest some useful courses of action that might be taken to deal with these problems, and that it will indicate the kinds of continuing investigations that must be conducted if the capability to control pollution is to be improved over time.

This book endeavours to progress in a logical fashion from a definition of the pollution problem to an examination of the technologies, policies and institutional arrangements to control pollution and ending with concrete suggestions for dealing with the problems identified. Chapter 2 provides an overview of the pollution control problem in the Lower Fraser with a view to aiding the reader in understanding how the remaining contributions fit together.

Chapters 3, 4 and 5 are concerned with the current condition of the aquatic ecosystem and the sources of the pollutants that reach the river. In Chapter 3, Ken Hall assesses water quality conditions in the river itself and identifies the major sources of the pollutants reaching the waterway. In Chapter 4, Ken Hall and John Wiens examine water quality conditions in selected tributaries of the Lower Fraser. They also identify pollution sources. Then in Chapter 5 Tom Northcote describes the biology of the Lower Fraser, indicates the effects pollution is having upon organisms in the river, and assesses the possible effects of future waste discharges upon the biology of the river.

Anthony Dorcey in Chapter 6, turns to the technologies of reducing pollution and the kinds of policies that might be employed to limit waste discharges to the aquatic environment. In Chapter 7 Mark Sproule-Jones and Ken Peterson focus on the institutional arrangements for pollution control. They portray the key features of this quite intricate system, identify its limitations and examine some ways of strengthening it.

The concluding Chapter undertakes the most difficult task faced in this study, namely the presentation of suggestions for controlling pollution more effectively in the Lower Fraser in light of the problems that have been uncovered through the Centre's research effort. What society considers to be the right course of action depends upon how it ranks its preferences and what risks it is willing to take in view of the uncertainties that exist. The course adopted with regard to pollution control depends upon the value society places upon protecting the resource in comparison with the value it places on other social objectives. What society considers appropriate to do may, for example, depend upon whether it prefers to use tax money to reduce the flow of toxic pollutants to the river and thus reduce the risks of adversely affecting the ecology of the river and the Strait of Georgia or whether it wishes to use tax money for some other purpose, such as the building of a new street or bridge. In offering specific suggestions in the concluding chapter we have assumed that the public and its governmental representatives give high priority to the preservation of water quality in the Lower Fraser. Our proposals are based on the premise that they will wish to take steps and make investments which reduce the risk to human health and aquatic ecosystems caused by current and prospective levels of waste discharge to the Lower Fraser River system. Fortunately the cost of such action is not very great.

2

The Problem in Perspective

by Irving K. Fox

The general purpose of this chapter is to provide an overview of the problem of controlling pollution in the Lower Fraser. First, it reviews the ways in which the Lower Fraser is used and examines the implications of these uses for the control of pollution. Then to provide a framework for understanding how the remaining chapters fit together, the major components of what we call the pollution control system are described.

THE LOWER FRASER AND ITS USES

The Lower Fraser is but a part of the Fraser River system which is one of the great river systems of North America. In average flow (96,000 cfs at Hope) it is the third largest in the country; in size of drainage (80,000 square miles) it ranks sixth. The Lower Fraser system — the drainage area below Hope — constitutes only 8 percent of the total drainage of the Fraser River system. The Lower Fraser has a number of important tributaries. The Harrison and others that flow from the north as well as the Chilliwack from the south drain forested mountain areas, while still others, such as the Salmon, drain agricultural land and exurban development, while the Brunette drains an urban-industrial area. An important natural feature of the river is that it carries a heavy load of sediment, which is responsible for its muddy appearance. Also, it is noteworthy that the influence of Fraser River flows extend well out into the Strait of Georgia and around into English Bay. To see the problem of water pollution control in the Lower Fraser in perspective one must examine how the quality of the river's water fits into the lives of the people of British Columbia and in particular into the lives of the people of the Lower Mainland.

Doug Miller

A million and a quarter people live in the Lower Fraser Valley and lands closely adjoining it. Virtually all of these people use the river in one way or another. A great many of them engage in economic activities that depend upon the river directly. For example, the forest industry uses it for the transport and storage of logs. The river provides harbour, port facilities, and a navigation channel for much of the commerce that flows through the Vancouver region. It provides water supplies for industries located on its banks and it supplies gravel from its bed for construction activities. It supports a greater salmon run than any river in the world, except the Yukon. On the average 300 million juvenile salmon migrate down the river to the sea in even years, and about 10 million adults migrate upstream annually to spawn. This enormous salmon run provides the basis for a major commercial fishing industry. Another use of the river that is of significant economic importance is that of providing a waste receptable for the sewage produced by most of the industries and households of the region and the runoff from urban and rural lands.

To serve these commercial demands the river has been "developed" in a variety of ways. Artificial spawning areas for the salmon have been developed in upstream tributary areas. The river is dredged and training works have been built to maintain the navigation channel. Dykes have been built to protect from flooding the rich farming land of the valley and the urban-industrial developments of the Greater Vancouver region. Sewage treatment plants have been constructed to reduce the potential pollution of waste discharges.

But beyond these commercial uses of the river, it serves the people of the Lower Mainland in other important ways. The salmon run which is the basis for a major commercial fishing industry also supports a very large sport fishing activity and the lower river provides the space for many of the marinas that serve this activity. It offers resting and feeding areas for an enormous population of migratory birds that follow the Pacific flyway and desirable habitat for many resident species of birds and mammals. The hunting and observation of wildlife, bar fishing, picnicking and walking on the banks of the river, and use of the beaches in the lower reaches makes the river a major recreation resource for the people of the Lower Mainland.

The uses made of the river and its associated lands are of tremendous value to the people of the Lower Mainland, but the river is something more than the foundation of economic activity. It is a feature of the physical-biological environment that is of immense psychological importance to the people of the Lower Fraser Valley. To the man fishing from a bar, to the person watching waterfowl in the marshes, to the child paddling in a pool, the river adds a richness to life that is difficult to measure. It is a link that people have with the complex ecological system of which they are a part. And along with the mountains and the sea it is the essence of this region of British Columbia and it is part of what people mean when they call it home. Thus, to many people, preserving the character of the river is something with which they associate the quality of life. These values cannot be measured through techniques of benefit-cost analysis but one of our studies did provide a small insight into the

Bar fishing near Mission.   Finn Larsen

importance of values of this kind. A few years ago New Westminster imposed a tax of $50.00 per household to defray the cost of sewage collection and treatment. A sample survey of New Westminster residents by Westwater indicated that more than half of those interviewed would be willing to pay even more than the tax to upgrade the treatment of sewage beyond the planned level.

This question of values leads to the essence of the problem of pollution control. The river provides services that are of great commercial importance — services that generally can be measured in jobs and dollars of income. Some of these commercial uses tend to degrade the water environment unless investments are made in pollution control measures. Such investments result in a reduction in income to some users, and depending upon the circumstances control of pollution may mean either an increase or a reduction in jobs. Thus pollution control involves a making of choices — a balancing of values between using the river for waste disposal to save income for some people and managing our wastes so that water quality is not degraded.

These are difficult choices, because the waste dischargers are not limited to a few sources that can be readily controlled. The dischargers are all the households that discharge sewage into the river. They are the motorists whose exhausts produce chemical fallout which eventually reaches the river. They are the home gardners whose pesticides wash into the storm sewers. They are the thousands of commercial establishments that use materials which eventually find their way into storm sewers and sanitary sewers and eventually end up in the river. The choices are difficult because the issues are not clear cut. It is seldom if ever a simple choice between the immediate destruction of an organism—like a fish kill—and withholding a pollutant from the river. Instead most frequently it is a choice between continuing to discharge pollutants thereby risking adversely affecting an aquatic ecosystem over the long term and keeping costs down, and reducing the discharge of pollutants but at a higher cost to society.

It is a choice in which the costs of pollution control can be estimated with reasonable accuracy and in which the benefits are much less certain because it is so difficult to estimate precisely what the effects of continued waste discharge will be upon the aquatic ecosystem. Our research does not say what choices should be made but it does indicate the kinds of choices we face and the consequences and uncertainties associated with alternative courses of action.

THE WATER POLLUTION CONTROL SYSTEM

With this general characterization of the problem in mind, let us examine more closely what can be called the water pollution control system. This system may be thought of as being composed of three sub-systems namely:

1. The Aquatic Ecosystem
2. The Waste Production Sub-System and
3. The Institutional Sub-System

Let us examine each of these sub-systems briefly to indicate how they relate to one another and to see what they tell us about the factors we must deal with if we are to control pollution effectively.

Suction dredge near Sea Island.   Public Works of Canada

The Aquatic Ecosystem

Without going into how an aquatic ecosystem functions it is important to recall some of its characteristics that are relevant to the management of water quality.

First, as is generally recognized, an ecosystem under natural conditions is composed of organisms which interact with one another and with their physical environment to achieve an approximate state of equilibrium. Within the system, populations increase and decline in response to changes in natural phenomena and frequently these changes are large, but throughout there is a tendency toward homeostasis. Man has learned to modify these natural systems to serve his special interests through, for example, fisheries enhancement programmes and aquaculture. He also disturbs these natural systems in a variety of other ways as illustrated by Table 1. As is evident from this table, the ecosystem may be altered in a number of ways. Our research has been concerned with only one of these ways, namely the effects of discharging materials to the water environment. We should not lose sight of the fact that the health of the aquatic ecosystem may be seriously impaired by means other than pollution.

Table I

WAYS IN WHICH MAN ALTERS THE AQUATIC ECOSYSTEM

I.   *By changing the physical structure of the environment through:*
     — construction of dykes and training works
     — dredging
     — construction of docks and marinas
     — withdrawing water for municipal, industrial, and irrigation purposes
     — altering the flow regime by building dams or changing vegetative cover

II. *By changing the number of organisms in the water by:*
     — fishing
     — hatchery and planting activities
     — hunting

III. *By increasing or decreasing the materials that reach the water through:*
     — disposal of wastes by industries, households, and boats
     — placing substances on the land that can be washed by rain into a waterway (fertilizers, pesticides, oils, etc.)
     — changing land use so as to modify the amount of erosion
     — fallout from air pollution

Pollution may affect the aquatic ecosystem in several ways:
1. It may alter the microbiology of water. Here our major concern is with an increase in pathogenic organisms that cause disease in human beings.

2. The chemical character of the water may be changed, which can make water toxic to both human beings and other organisms. Also, the temperature of water may be elevated.

3. The transparency of water may be affected which in turn influences photosynthetic processes.

4. The foregoing factors may combine to alter the kind, number, and growth of organisms.

5. Some forms of pollution may give water an unattractive appearance which reduces its aesthetic and recreation value.

Figure 1 illustrates an important feature of the aquatic ecosystem with regard to pollution. This figure indicates how a very low concentration of a toxic material in water becomes magnified as it moves up the food chain so that the concentration in fish at the top of the food chain may be 10,000 times the concentration in water. The reason for this magnification of the concentration is illustrated by Figure 2. As it moves up the food chain the same quantity of toxic

BIO-MAGNIFICATION OF PERSISTENT

TOXIC MATERIAL

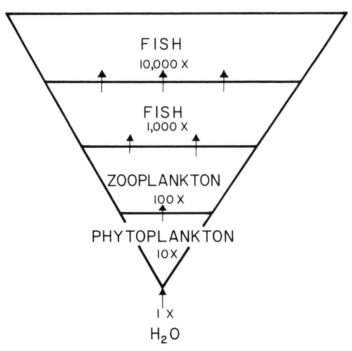

Figure 1

RELATIVE BIOMASS OF TROPHIC LEVELS OF AQUATIC FOODCHAIN

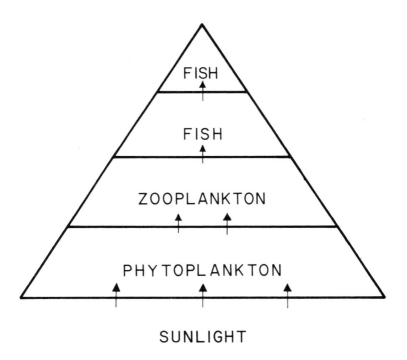

Figure 2

material becomes concentrated in a much smaller biomass since each trophic level must live off the trophic level immediately below and the upper level must consume a much larger biomass than itself to be sustained. People tend to use organisms at the top of the food chain for food.

A final point with regard to the effects of pollution on the aquatic ecosystem is that most forms of pollution cause the diversity of species to decline as pollution increases. A reduction in diversity reduces the resilience of an ecosystem and indicates a decline in its health. A substantial part of Westwater's research funds have been invested in trying to understand the condition of the Lower Fraser's aquatic ecosystem and a full report on what has been learned is provided in Chapters 3, 4 and 5.

POLLUTION PATHWAYS

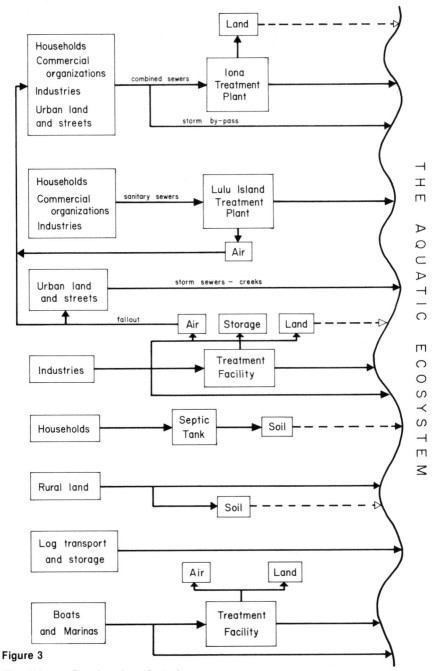

Figure 3

The Waste Production Sub-System

The Waste Production Sub-System is the second component of the Pollution Control System that we will consider. Figure 3 is designed to convey some

understanding of how wastes—those materials which we cannot use econo-
mically—find their way into the river and become pollutants.

The figure illustrates a number of important points:

First, there are a number of different pathways by which pollutants reach the
river. Not only is effluent discharged from treatment plants, but in addition:

— Waste water runs off urban land and streets through storm sewers and
  creeks.
— Some industries discharge effluents directly to the river.
— Wastes may seep to the waterway from septic tanks.
— There is runoff from rural land.
— Bark and other materials are deposited in the river in the course of trans-
  porting and storing logs.
— Boats and marinas may discharge wastes to the river.

While some pathways contribute much more waste than others, we cannot
ignore the fact that in a complex metropolitan region pollutants reach the
river from a large number of discrete sources.

Second, since storm sewers and sanitary sewers are combined in much of
Vancouver, the Iona treatment plant which handles them cannot handle all of
the effluent it receives during a heavy rain. Thus, it must bypass without treatment some of the sewage it receives during a storm.

Third, treatment processes invariably produce a residual—or sludge—which
must be disposed of in some way:

— If this residual is disposed of by putting it on the land it may leach through
  the soil to the waterway.
— If it is incinerated, materials are discharged to the atmosphere which become fall-out and again can be washed into the waterway.

Care must be exercised in the disposal of the residual from treatment plants if
we are in fact to limit the adverse effects of environmental pollution.

Figure 4 helps to clarify the points in the sub-system where action can be taken
to reduce the discharge of pollutants to the Lower Fraser.

The figure indicates that pollutants may be collected from household,
commercial and industrial establishments and then treated and discharged to a
waterway. These are referred to as "point sources" of pollution. However, a
substantial contributor to pollution are the "non point sources". This is the
runoff from agricultural land, forest land, home gardens, roads and streets
which reaches the river in a wide variety of ways. The figure also illustrates that
the quantity and quality of the wastes that reach the river from households and
industrial establishments can be influenced in a number of ways:

1. The materials used by a household or industry can be controlled, e.g. the
   use of a toxic material might be prohibited.

2. An industry may treat its wastes and recycle all or a portion of them, or
   remove the harmful parts and discharge them to the land, to the atmosphere through incineration or put them into storage.

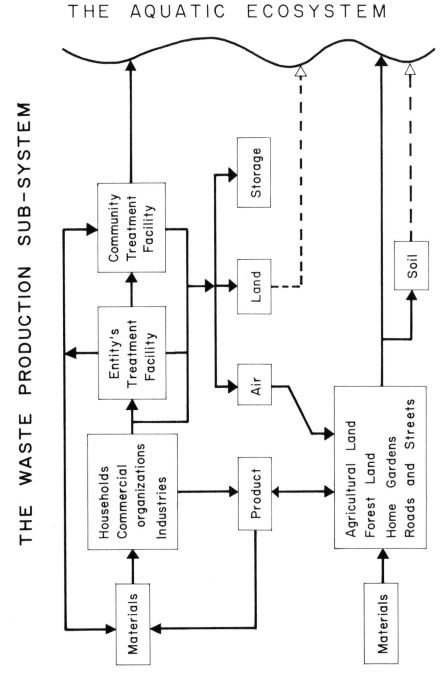

Figure 4

3. An industry may pipe its wastes to a community treatment facility which in turn may treat the wastes, recover some materials for recycling and/or transform some of the wastes into a harmless form, and/or discharge some of the wastes to the land, to the atmosphere or to storage.

Similarly for those wastes that come from streets, gardens, forests and farmlands, control can be exercised (a) by reducing or eliminating the use of polluting materials, (b) by preventing the materials from flowing off the land into the river or (c) by collecting the waste water and resorting to a treatment process which results in the recovery of some materials, transforming some wastes into a harmless form and/or permitting the isolation of harmful wastes so that they cannot cause damage.

In concluding this discussion of the waste production sub-system there are three points that should be made.

First, even if treatment plants in the Lower Fraser Valley are upgraded so that all significant pollutants are removed from their effluents, two problems will remain. One is that major quantities of pollutants do not enter sewers that lead to treatment plants but flow directly into the river system, and these are significant discharges. For example Ken Hall's investigations as described in Chapter 3 indicate that the major source of lead pollution is urban runoff and a major part of urban runoff never flows to a treatment plant. The other problem that will remain if a high level of treatment is achieved is that the toxic materials removed through treatment must be put somewhere. If they are put on the land the chances are that at least some will leach through the soil and reach the waterway; if incinerated they will become fall-out, return to the land and thence move to the waterway.

Second, we must be cautious about using sewage effluents to irrigate and fertilize gardens, lawns, forests and agricultural crops. Since chemicals are so widely used in households, commercial establishments, and industries, sewage effluents contain toxic materials such as heavy metals. If these effluents are applied to land there is a possibility that toxic materials will build up in the soil, contaminate ground water supplies, or move through the ground to a surface stream.

Third, in view of the problem of controlling and disposing of toxic materials once they become pollutants we should give a great deal of thought to controlling them at their source. If, for example, we can keep lead out of gasoline, we will not face the costly problem of trying to control it when it runs off streets and land areas along highways. Furthermore, if toxic pollutants can be kept out of sewage, use of sewage effluents as fertilizer will become a much more practical disposal alternative than it now is.

Chapter 6 will be devoted to an examination of the specific nature of the Waste Production sub-system and the technologies that might be utilized to limit the production of wastes and control discharges to the aquatic environment.

The Institutional Sub-System

The third critical component of the Pollution Control System is what may be termed the Institutional Sub-System. Societal control over the discharge of pollutants is effected largely through the instruments of government — laws, regulations, taxes, subsides, and agencies. The institutional sub-system is made up of these instruments of government and their application to individuals and public and private organizations. We call it a "system" to connote the complex interacting of a wide diversity of interests through which it operates. The purpose of the institutional sub-system is to act upon the waste production sub-system to achieve the greatest benefits from our use of the aquatic ecosystem. Many observers assert that the only certain way to achieve the greatest benefits is to invest authority and capability in a single agency and let it prescribe the right courses of action for waste producers. Chapters 6 and 7 will discuss this question in more detail but Figure 5 illustrates one aspect of the institutional sub-system as it exists now and indicates something of its complexity and diversity. It suggests that the vesting of authority in a single agency may not be as simple a solution as it first appears to be.

When a potential discharger decides to apply to the Pollution Control Branch of B.C. for a permit to discharge its wastes to the Lower Fraser the following series of steps are initiated within a very few days: usually a consulting engineer is hired to help fill in the requisite forms; the Pollution Control Branch upon receipt of the application forwards copies, as required by the Pollution Control Act, to four provincial agencies
— the Comptroller of Water Rights
— the Deputy Minister of Recreation and Travel Industry
— the Minister of Health and
— the Deputy Minister of Agriculture.
Also, as has become customary, a copy is forwarded to the Environmental Protection Service of Environment Canada. If the discharger is an industry within a municipality then the municipal engineer is furnished a copy. A copy of the application is also published in the B.C. Gazette which is monitored by wildlife and conservation groups.

Each of the groups initially informed passes the information on to others. The Environmental Protection Service notifies fisheries operations of the Federal Fisheries Service, which in turn asks for comments from its field officers, from the fisheries research agencies, and from the International Pacific Salmon Fisheries Commission. The Provincial agencies notify their field offices, and the central wildlife and conservation offices inform member groups in whose region the application has been made. Also notified are those who have an interest in the specific property involved because of an adjacent water license or pollution control permit.

Each of these entities may make representations to the Pollution Control Branch on the application for discharge to the degree it is motivated to do so by the extent to which its interests will be affected. Figure 5 does not indicate the amount of communication among the groups of similar interest in their attempts

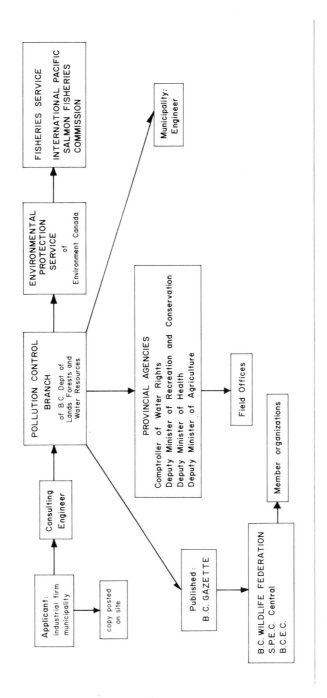

Figure 5 Applications for a permit to discharge wastes circulate through several agencies.

to influence the nature of the permit to be issued, or indeed the issuance of any permit at all. As most people are aware, if some party feels that its interests are vitally affected it not only makes representations to the Pollution Control Branch but it also solicits information and support from other parties whose interest might be affected. It should also be pointed out that while the Pollution Control Branch is officially at the centre of the permit granting process, the other entities are not without powers of their own. The Federal agencies have the authority of the Fisheries Act to sustain them; provincial agencies can appeal under terms provided in the Pollution Control Act or in some cases under the more sweeping terms of the Environment and Land Use Act; the wildlife and conservation groups have sizable constituencies which public agencies can only ignore at thier peril.

It is not the purpose of this essay to comment on the appropriateness or effectiveness of the procedure now followed. But this simple illustration of one part of our institutional sub-system serves to illustrate the wide range of interests that must be taken into account in decisions about controlling pollution. If it is recognized that these are legitimate interests which have a right to participate in the decision-making process, how could a single agency or authority simplify the procedure without impairing what we have come to consider as essential elements of our democratic processes? Without attempting here to answer this question, this example may help to clarify the nature of the institutional problem that must be addressed.

In brief then the institutional sub-system seeks to reflect the will of society — a summing up of the preferences of its many members in accord with rules that have evolved over centuries. This sub-system then seeks to impose that will upon the dischargers of wastes to the aquatic environment. When we are concerned about improving the institutional sub-system we are seeking a way of making it reflect the will of society more faithfully and to implement the choices that are made more effectively and efficiently.

The Relationship Among the Three Sub-Systems

The general relationships by which the three sub-systems are connected to one another are illustrated by Figure 6. Simply stated the Institutional Sub-system learns from the Waste Production Sub-system about the production of wastes, how discharges of wastes might be controlled, and what some of the conse-quences of control would be for components of the production process. The Institutional Sub-system also learns from examination of the Aquatic Ecosystem what the consequences of discharging wastes to the water environment are likely to be. On the basis of this information the Institutional Sub-system takes implementing action, which, if effective keeps the discharge of wastes to the aquatic environment to the desired levels.

The type of implementing actions to be utilized require careful thought and study. What steps can we take to limit the use of toxic materials if we decide that this should be done? For example, should the use of leaded gasoline be banned or should leaded gasoline be heavily taxed? Today the use of leaded gasoline is

THE POLLUTION CONTROL SYSTEM

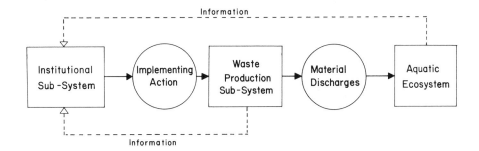

Figure 6

encouraged because it is cheaper than the unleaded. Can we expect small industrial users of heavy metals and other toxic materials to keep their effluents out of sewers unless they are provided with other means of disposal? These critical questions will be examined more fully in Chapter 6.

SUMMARY AND CONCLUSIONS

In conclusion I wish to draw your attention to the theme of this volume, namely the uncertain future of the Lower Fraser.

Our studies indicate that today the water quality of the Lower Fraser is surprisingly good when compared with other heavily used rivers of the world and in spite of the amounts and kinds of wastes we are discharging into it. But our studies also reveal a dark cloud on the horizon—unmistakeable evidence that abnormal quantities of toxic substances are accumulating in the organisms of the river's ecosystem. What will the effects be if these discharges continue into the future—especially if the rate of discharge increases as the result of the enormous growth of population and economic activity projected for the Lower Mainland? While accurate estimates of the likely consequences cannot be made, there can be little doubt that the risks of inaction or half-measures are large. The issue we face is this:

Are we willing to make the investment and exercise the wisdom required to reduce the flow of pollutants to the river to a level that minimizes the risks of damage both now and in the future?

In the chapters which follow we endeavour to define more precisely the nature of the pollution control problem in the Lower Fraser and suggest specific steps to enhance the quality of the river's waters and minimize the risks of future damage.

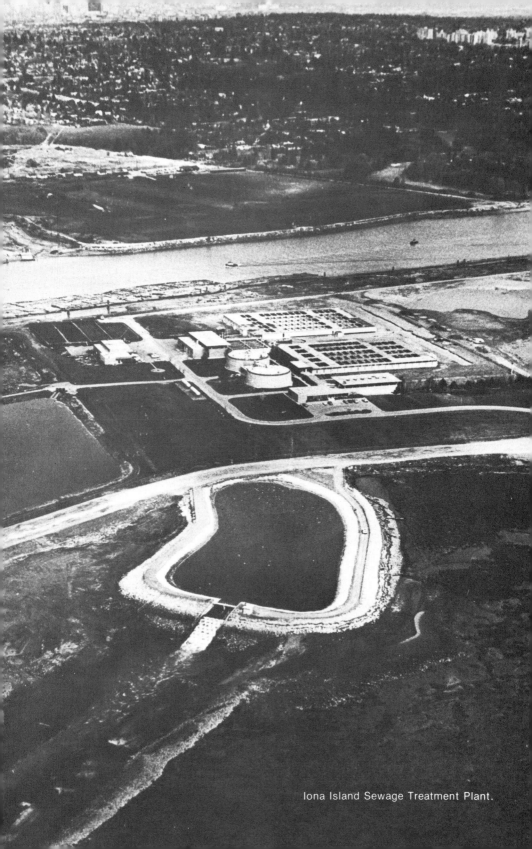

Iona Island Sewage Treatment Plant.

3

The Quality of Water in the Lower Fraser River and Sources of Pollution

by Kenneth J. Hall

Greater Vancouver Sewerage and Drainage District.

In chapter 2 of this volume the impacts of pollution on the aquatic ecosystem are discussed. In this chapter and Chapter 4 these impacts are examined in more detail and two basic questions are addressed, namely,

1. What are present water quality conditions in the Lower Fraser system?
2. What are the sources of pollutants?

Studies were undertaken by Westwater to seek the answer to these two questions because there was insufficient information available to determine either the extent and nature of the pollution or the capabilities that would be required by management to control this pollution.

The water quality investigations conducted in the Lower Fraser extended from Hope to the Strait of Georgia (Figure 1). In addition to stations on the main stem of the river, several tributaries, including the Harrison, Chilliwack, Sumas, Salmon, and Brunette River systems were studied to determine the effects of land use and local activities on water quality. This chapter is devoted to the water quality studies of the mainstem while the studies of water quality in the tributaries are discussed in Chapter 4.

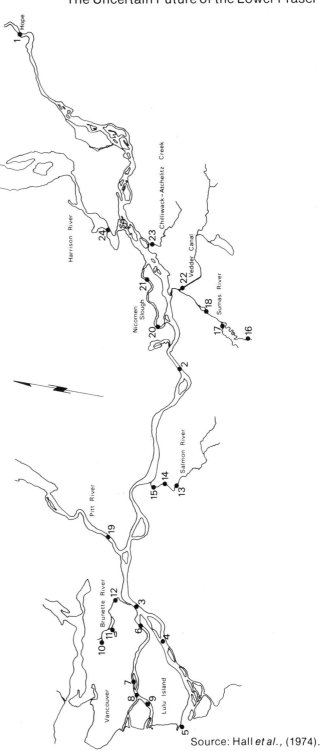

Fraser River and Tributary Sampling Sites

Figure 1

Source: Hall *et al.*, (1974).

WATER QUALITY

When one wants to measure the pollution level in an aquatic ecosystem there are several parameters or groups of factors that can be measured. These include:

1. Oxygen
2. Pathogen Indicator Organisms
3. Nutrients
4. Trace Metals
5. Chlorinated Hydrocarbons
6. Other toxic substances

The concentration of these parameters in the water, sediment and biota of the river, provides an indication of the condition of the ecosystem. This chapter deals with the quality of the water and sediments. Information on pollutants in the biota is presented in Chapter 5.

When the concern is about *water* quality why is it necessary to study the sediments? Since many of the substances discharged to waterways are very water insoluble, they tend to associate readily with the particulate materials in water and ultimately become part of the sediments. Such materials include trace metals, chlorinated hydrocarbons, and some nutrients such as phosphorus. These contaminants would not cause problems if they remained in the sediments and were covered by successive sedimentation; however, under some conditions they can again be released to the water or picked up by organisms living in close association with the river bottom.

Each one of these water quality parameters is discussed in the following pages to assess its level in the Lower Fraser and determine how its level is affecting the aquatic biota and the use of this water resource by man. Detailed data are available in Technical Report No. 4 (Hall *et al.,* 1974).

Oxygen and BOD

High concentrations of oxygen are required in water in order to provide a healthy habitat for fish and other biota. However, when domestic sewage or other degradable organic matter is discharged to the water an oxygen demand is exerted in which microorganisms use oxygen to degrade the organic matter by the following reaction -

$$\text{ORGANIC MATTER} + O_2 \xrightarrow{\text{MICROBES}} CO_2 + H_2O + \text{ENERGY}$$

The potential of this organic matter to consume oxygen is known as the *B*iochemical *O*xygen *D*emand or simply BOD. In addition to the BOD, oxygen levels can also be affected by temperature, dissolved salts, photosynthesis, water turbulence and oxidizable inorganic materials.

What are the oxygen and BOD conditions of the Lower Fraser? In brief, they appear to be very good in the main stem of the river. Oxygen concentrations are most often near the saturation level and BOD is usually low, near the detection limit of 1-2 mg/l. Although the river has received enormous amounts of

AVERAGE DISSOLVED OXYGEN LEVELS

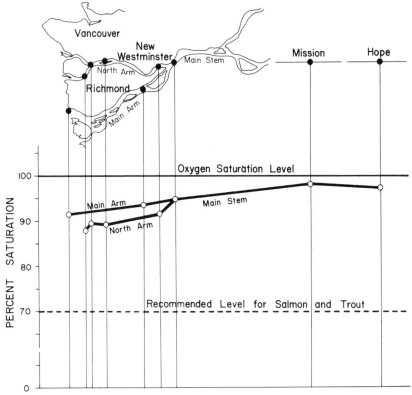

Figure 2   Source: Hall *et al.*, (1974).

untreated organic wastes which have been dumped into it, due to the amount of
dilution taking place its capacity to handle these degradable organics is
large, — almost analogous to a drop in a bucket of water. A slight decrease in the
average saturation value is apparent as one proceeds downstream from Hope,
with the lowest values being recorded in the North and Middle Arms of the river
(Figure 2). Therefore, it is apparent that some initial oxygen depletion is taking
place but saturation values are still high enough for the safe movement of salmon
and other aquatic organisms in the river. For example, the lowest saturation
values represent 9 to 10 mg/l oxygen (85% saturation), and it is recommended
that a level of 7.8 mg/l oxygen (approximately 70% saturation) would provide a
high level of protection to trout (FWPCF, 1968).

Pathogen Indicator Microorganisms

In order to indicate the presence of waterborn pathogens such as *Salmonella,*
Shigella, and *Cholera,* it is customary to measure a group of bacteria known as
coliforms. The reason for measuring these indicator mircoorganisms is that they
occur in fairly large numbers, are much easier to culture in the laboratory, and

Fraser Main Arm looking west toward Deas Tunnel. Annacis Island lower right.
David LeMarquand

there is a fairly good statistical relationship between the presence of these indicators and the actual pathogens.

From the information presented in Figure 3 it is readily apparent that there is an increase in the numbers of total coliforms as one proceeds downstream and that levels are much higher in the North Arm of the river than in the Main Arm.

In addition to total coliforms there are two other groups of organisms, namely fecal coliforms and fecal streptococci, which serve as pathogen indicators and provide a very crude means of determining whether the source of fecal contamination is human or animal wastes. Both of these groups of micro-organisms also have higher numbers in the lower reaches of the Fraser. What do these levels mean in terms of our safe use of this water resource? Table 1 compares acceptable fecal coliform levels used as guidelines for water use to the average values for the Fraser River stations. At Hope, with numbers as high as 490 organisms/100 ml, the water is almost unacceptable as a drinking water source. At Mission, the bacteriological quality has deteriorated further so that the water cannot be used for drinking and in some cases would be dangerous for primary contact recreation such as swimming. Moving downstream to the Main Arm stations, at Annacis and Garry Point the water becomes only marginally acceptable for non-contact recreation and irrigation, and conditions in the North Arm are so bad that the water cannot be used for non-contact recreation or irrigation purposes. These data were collected prior to construction of the Annacis Island Sewage Treatment Plant which intercepts many previously direct discharges, so there should now be some improvement in the bacteriological water quality. However, large numbers of coliform microorganisms also come from storm runoff so Annacis will not likely solve the problem completely.

TABLE 1

FECAL COLIFORMS IN THE LOWER FRASER

Station	Fecal Coliforms	Acceptable Water Use
HOPE	130	borderline drinking
MISSION	775	no drinking or swimming
PATULLO BR.	2750	no use
ANNACIS IS.	1130	marginally acceptable for non-contact recreation and irrigation
GARRY PT.	880	same as Annacis
QUEENSBORO BR.	7730	no use
FRASER ST.	16,480	no use
OAK ST.	5110	no use
DINSMORE BR.	2550	no use

Hall *et al.* (1974)

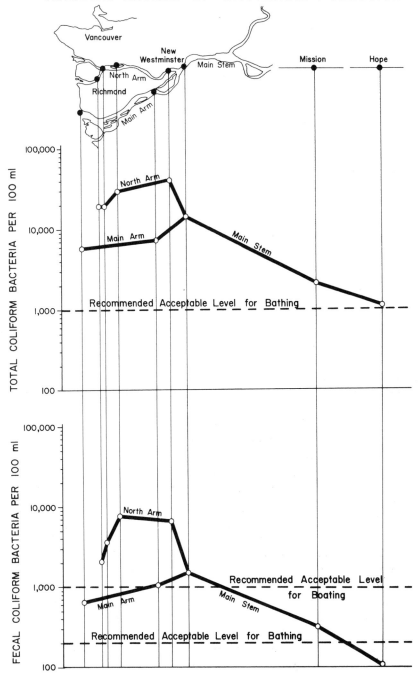

AVERAGE LEVELS OF BACTERIAL POLLUTION

Figure 3

Source: Hall *et al.*, (1974).

Nutrients

Nutrients usually refer to those substances which are necessary for healthy growth and can indeed stimulate growth if they are supplied to an environment where that nutrient is in a low supply. However too much nutrient enrichment, referred to as eutrophication, leads to increased growths of algae which, when they die, may exert an excessive oxygen demand upon the water resulting in detrimental effects upon other aquatic organisms such as fish. In the aquatic environment the two main nutrients of concern in this regard are usually nitrogen and phosphorus. The nutrient status in the Lower Fraser, however, looks very good. Concentrations of nitrogen and phosphorus are in general quite low when compared to many other river systems in North America. Between Hope and the Strait of Georgia no increase in average nutrient concentrations is apparent which could be associated with man's activities in the Lower Fraser Valley. Although the Fraser Valley does deliver a nutrient load to the Strait of Georgia, concentrations of nitrogen and phosphorus in the river itself are lower than those in the Strait, especially in the winter time. However, it must be pointed out that the effects of nutrients in the Fraser on productivity are very difficult to interpret from relative concentrations, since the availability of these nutrients to the biota is often difficult to assess.

An important factor influencing the transport of nutrients and other parameters in the Fraser is the flow regime. During spring and summer runoff, when flow in the Lower Fraser can increase by more than a factor of 10, erosion occurring in the river basin causes large quantities of sediment to be transported to the Strait of Georgia. Associated with this sediment are large amounts of nutrients, such as phosphorus, and other materials, such as iron (Figure 4). Although some of this sediment transport may be attributable to logging and agricultural practices, which cause erosion in the upper basin, most of it probably results from natural erosion processes.

Even if excess amounts of nutrients were discharged to the Fraser, the water is generally too turbid for light to penetrate and excessive growths of algae to occur, although excessive nutrients could result in greater quantities of attached algae that grow on logs and exposed mud flats or aquatic plants growing in shallow areas of the river.

Toxicity

The last three sets of water quality parameters to be discussed here are trace metals, chlorinated hydrocarbons and other toxic substances such as hydrocarbons and phenols. They have one characteristic in common, namely most of them possess toxic properties.

Time magazine (Oct. 20, 1975) has described trace metals and other toxic pollutants escaping to our environment as the disease of the century. However, cases like the blatant evidence of Minimata disease, where industrial discharges of mercury killed an estimated 300 people and crippled many others for life, are the exception rather than the rule. Most of the so-called diseases caused by environmental contaminants are of a more subtle nature and it is very difficult to establish the cause-effect relationships.

SEASONAL CHANGE IN DISCHARGE AND WATER QUALITY

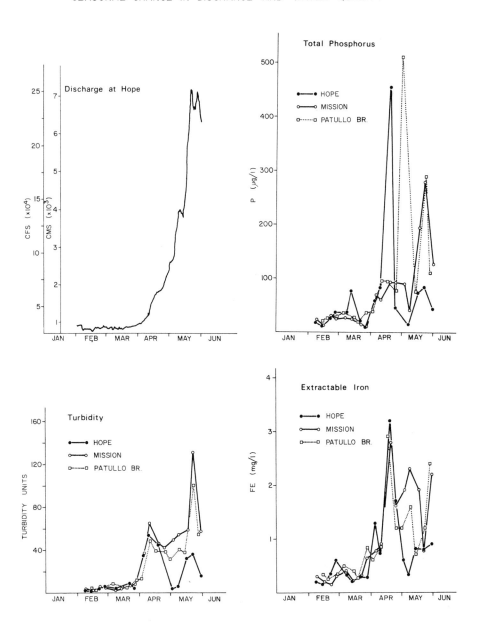

Figure 4   Source: Hall *et al.*, (1974).

There are three aspects of toxicity which are very important for an understanding of this complex subject.

First, it is important to delineate two forms of toxicity, namely *acute* and *chronic*. Acute toxicity is caused by higher concentrations of toxic materials and results in a fairly rapid death of the organism affected. Chronic toxicity is a long term toxicity caused by low levels of toxicants, which may or may not result in the direct death of the organism. It affects functions such as reproduction, feeding efficiency, behaviour and other important processes.

A second aspect, already described in Chapter 1, but worth repeating here, is the ability of organisms to concentrate pollutants in their systems by the process of food chain concentration, where a concentration of 1x in the water is magnified to several 1000x by the time it reaches the top organism on the food pyramid—a direct result of the large amounts of food necessary to sustain the top organism.

A third and equally important aspect of toxicity is direct absorption by the organism. A good example of this is provided by shellfish, which must process large quantities of water to obtain their food. Since the pollutants involved are not very soluble in water they tend to accumulate in the tissues of the organism and become concentrated there.

A final point that should be made about toxic materials is that their level of toxicity is affected by other quality parameters such as temperature, oxygen, suspended solids and hardness in the water. For example, a given concentration of trace metals will be more toxic if the water is very soft. Also, high temperatures increase the metabolic activity of an organism making a given concentration of trace metal more toxic at a higher temperature.

Trace Metals

Trace metals that have been considered toxic in the aquatic environment include silver (Ag), arsenic (As), cadmium (Cd), chromium (Cr), copper (Cu), mercury (Hg), nickel (Ni), lead (Pb), selenium (Se), and zinc (Zn), although it should be kept in mind that all of these elements occur naturally and most organisms need at least some of these in trace amounts for their healthy growth. It is when discharges of trace metals exceed the levels with which the aquatic environment has evolved that symptoms of toxicity begin to occur.

TABLE 2	TRACE METALS (WATER)[1]		
STATION	Copper	Mercury	Lead	Zinc
Fraser River	3	< .05	< 1	6
(Hope)	(< 1 - 9)	(< .05- < .05)	(< 1 - 4)	(1 - 20)
Main Arm-Fraser River	4	< .05	< 1	5
(Annacis Island)	(< 1 - 8)	(< .05 - .35)	(< 1 - 1)	(< 1 - 70)
North Arm-Fraser River	4	< .05	< 1	10.5
(Fraser Street)	(< 1 - 6)	(< .05 - .24)	(< 1 - 3)	(< 1 - 80)

1. All metals presented as medians and ranges in ug/litre.
Hall *et al.*, (1974).

In the Lower Fraser, the *median* values for four of these metals, namely copper, mercury, lead and zinc do not differ greatly in upstream (Hope) and downstream (Main and North Arm) concentrations, with the possible exception of zinc in the North Arm of the river (Table 2). However, the range of concentrations for mercury, lead and zinc shows an increase in the range of values in the lower reaches of the river adjacent to metropolitan Vancouver (Figure 5). This indicates that a sporadic discharge of these toxic substances occurs in the reaches of the river below Pattullo Bridge.

TRACE METAL CONCENTRATIONS

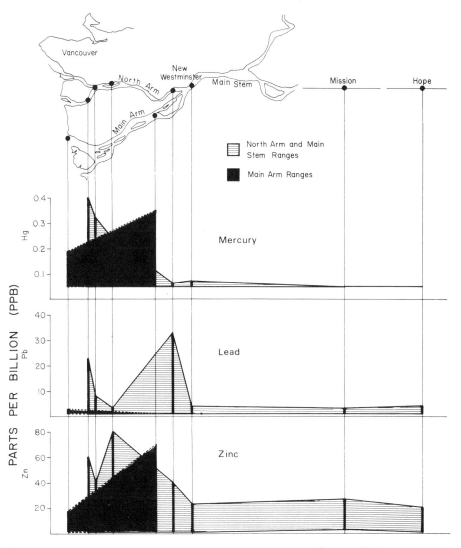

Figure 5   Source: Hall *et al.*, (1974).

What do these concentrations mean for the use of the Fraser and what is their toxicity to the aquatic biota? In terms of use of the river for drinking water, for example, the only toxic metal that exceeds the standards that have been set is mercury. It is fair to say that the levels of coliforms pose a more serious problem than trace metals in considering the Fraser as a drinking water source.

It is not easy to determine the toxicity to fish and other aquatic biota of these concentrations of trace metals because our present understanding of toxicity is so fragmentary. Further, the toxicity of a given trace metal will depend upon the species of fish, its age, its life history, the availability of the metal to the fish, the other metals and pollutants present. However, if the data on trace metal levels in the Fraser are compared to some of the lowest toxic concentrations cited in the literature (Cd, 3ug/l; Cu, 10ug/l; Hg, 5ug/l; Pb, 10ug/l, and Zn, 10ug/l - Buhler, 1972) it is found that cadmium and mercury in the river never exceed these levels, copper and lead exceed them less than 3 percent of the time and 30 percent of the zinc values exceed the 10ug/l level (ug/l = parts per billion). However, this zinc concentration appears to be fairly close to the natural or unpolluted level for the Lower Fraser, so it is certainly not toxic to organisms which have evolved in this particular environment. Hence it is apparent that individual trace metal concentrations do not appear to cause significant acute toxicity to fish in the Fraser. If the toxicity of a combination of the metals copper, lead and zinc is considered, it will be found that the levels at all stations are below the average level at which some adverse effect upon the fish may occur (Figure 6). If, however, these levels are assessed for each set of sampling data, there are a few times when this so called 'safe level' is exceeded and this happens more frequently in the lower reaches of the river as shown by data from Queensboro Bridge (Figure 7). It must, however, be recognized that zinc appears to be the main metal responsible for exceeding this toxicity criterion and the literature values probably overstate the toxicity of this metal to Fraser fish. Hence, it is evident that trace metals in combination have a higher toxicity to fish than individually, and concentrations in the Lower Fraser appear to be reaching the threshold of harmful effect.

Most trace metals are not very soluble in water and usually become associated with particles and end up in the sediments. From the concentrations of copper, lead and zinc in Table 3 it is readily apparent that the discharge from the Iona sewage treatment plant is having an impact upon trace metals in the estuarine sediments of Sturgeon Banks. Sediments from Sturgeon Banks in the vicinity of the North Arm contain higher concentrations of lead than are found at Roberts Banks near the Main Arm, which compares favorably with the higher sporadic concentration of lead measured in North Arm waters. Ladner slough contains much higher trace metal levels than are found in the open channel of the river. This is an expected phenomenum since these backwater areas represent zones of sedimentation where the finer particles settle, and trace metals are generally associated with the finer particles; whereas the main channel of the river, which is scoured frequently by high flows, contains mostly coarse sand.

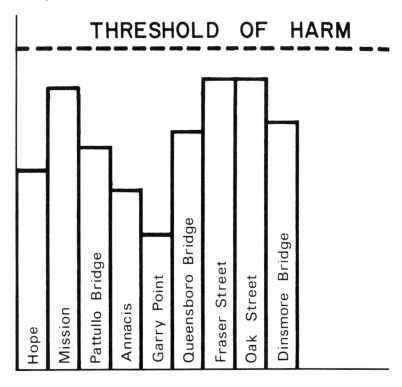

**AVERAGE TOXICITY OF COMBINATION
OF TRACE METALS (Cu, Pb, & Zn)
AT FRASER RIVER STATIONS**

Figure 6   Source: Hall *et al.*, (1974).

TABLE 3

TRACE METALS IN SEDIMENTS OF THE FRASER[1]

Area	Copper	Lead	Zinc
North Arm	34	16	72
Sturgeon Banks (Iona STP)	183	157	170
Roberts Banks	28	4	61
Main Arm	17-36	4-11	25-60
Ladner Slough	43-57	14-23	95-115

1. all values in mg/kg.
Hall and Fletcher (1974); Bourque and Adams (1975).

SEASONAL VARIATION IN TOXICITY

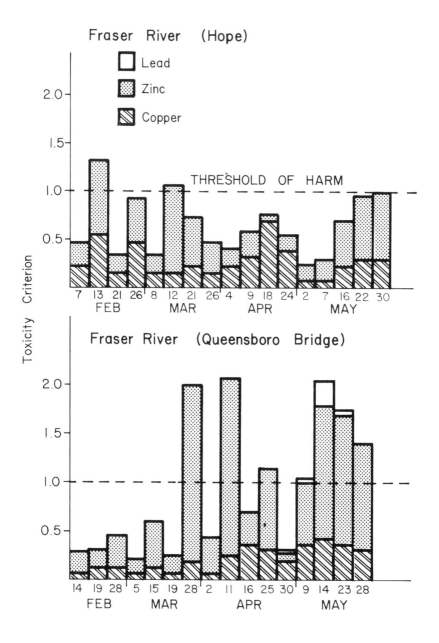

Figure 7   Source: Hall *et al.*, (1974).

What is the impact upon the biota of these higher levels of trace metals found in sediments? It is difficult to assess this impact since very little information is available on the exchange of trace metals with the water. However, it is expected that bottom feeding organisms, as they graze over the sediment particles, could pick up higher levels of trace metals and possibly pass them up the food chain.

Chlorinated Hydrocarbons

When the term chlorinated hydrocarbons is used, it refers to pesticides such as DDT and PCB's (polychlorinated biphenyls), which are organic compounds similar to pesticides containing chlorine and are used in a variety of products. The common characteristic of these chlorinated hydrocarbons is that they are very persistent (that is to say, they do not break down easily) and they are toxic. During our study, seventy water samples were collected for chlorinated hydrocarbon analysis. All samples from the Fraser River were below the detection limits for these materials. However, these results do not mean that there is no contamination in the Lower Fraser since these substances are very insoluble, and unless they were discharged close to the sampling site during the sampling period, they would be rapidly removed from the water and absorbed to the sediments. Owing to the expense involved, no chlorinated hydrocarbon determinations were made on the Fraser River sediments. However, some analyses were made on tributary sediments and these will be discussed in the next chapter.

Other Toxic Substances

On a couple of occasions samples were collected to measure other toxic substances such as phenols and hydrocarbons in Fraser River water, but concentrations were below the detection limit. From studies on sewage discharges we know that these materials are discharged to the river, but the great dilution capacity of the Fraser apparently dilutes them beyond detection or they are degraded fairly rapidly in the river. Other toxic compounds that have not been investigated include ammonia, surfactants such as detergents and a host of organic compounds that are used by our highly industrialized society.

EFFECT OF CHANGES IN DISCHARGES

What would happen to the existing concentrations of pollutants in the waters of the Lower Fraser that have just been described if waste discharges were changed or if there was a large accidental spill? To answer these questions it is necessary to know how the rate of dilution varies under different flow conditions. Through dye studies in the river actual dilution rates were measured for flow and tide conditions causing low dilution (Ward, 1975). In order to estimate rates of dilution under different flow and tide conditions a mathematical model was developed (Joy, 1975).

Two dye-tracer experiments, involving the dumping of a slug of dye, were conducted under different flow and tide conditions in the vicinity of Annacis Island Sewage Treatment Plant outfall. In both experiments there was a fairly rapid dilution of the dye, although it was several miles downstream before mixing occurred completely across the Main Arm. A subsequent study by B.C. Research, involving the continuous discharge of dye through one of the diffusers of the Annacis outfall, indicated similar rates of dilution (B.C. Research, 1975). This study was conducted under tide and flow conditions which B.C. Research characterized as "almost the worst possible situation for disposal of effluent into the Fraser River near Annacis Island" and it was found that the minimum instantaneous dilution was almost five fold. From this, the dye studies have indicated that, under similar conditions — i.e. when dilution rates are low, a pollutant would be diluted 10,000 times in 50 minutes, 100,000 times in 90-150 minutes and a million times in 300-350 minutes. Such information allows an estimation to be made of the effects of large accidental spills. For example, if a metric ton of copper ion spilled from a tank car directly into the river — that is an accident with an extremely large quantity of toxic pollutant — under these flow conditions, it would take 6-8 hours to reduce the concentration below that considered acutely toxic to rainbow trout.

The model that was developed has been used to estimate the effects of large discharges of BOD on dissolved oxygen concentrations in the river. It was found that even with a discharge of 1,000,000 pounds of BOD (equivalent to the raw domestic waste from a population of 5,000,000 people) in the vicinity of Chilliwack, levels would not be depressed enough to have any effect on fish survival in the main channels of the river.

SOURCES OF POLLUTANTS

In the first chapter it was pointed out that there are a host of different pathways by which pollutants can enter the Lower Fraser. There are point sources such as the sewage treatment plants and direct industrial discharges. There are non-point sources such as runoff from urban and agricultural areas. Within the sewage treatment plants there are sanitary wastes from residential areas, industrial discharges to the sewers and, in the case of combined systems, contributions from stormwater runoff. In an investigation of sources there are two important components to consider. One is the concentration of materials in the discharge that could be acutely toxic to the biota or affect some use of the water immediately downstream. The other factor is the flow or volume of discharge, since it is the concentration X flow which gives the load of chemical discharged to the waterway. This load and the dilution it receives in the river determine the ultimate concentration in the water and the resultant long term effects upon the biota or potential for food chain concentration.

Since adverse water quality conditions in the mainstem Fraser appear to be associated with the presence of pathogens and toxic substances such as trace metals and chlorinated hydrocarbons, this discussion of sources will consider only these quality parameters. Not very much information is available on the sources of chlorinated hydrocarbons since they were not considered to be a problem until some high concentrations were found in fish taken from the lower reaches of the river (Johnston *et al.,* 1975). Some evidence on how these materials enter the aquatic ecosystem will be discussed in the following chapter.

The first source of pollution that should be considered is the sewage from the treatment plants. Some perspective on the quality of sewage effluent can be obtained by comparison of pollutant concentrations in sewage to values found in the Fraser. Coliform organisms in the effluent are often one thousand or more times greater than the values recorded in the river. Nutrients, as represented by nitrogen and phosphorus, are 10-20 times greater in the sewage than the values reported in the river, and trace metals in the sewage may show values 100 times the lower values in the river. However, there tends to be considerable variation in the concentrations of all these parameters in both sewage and river water.

There are three sewage treatment plants in metropolitan Vancouver which discharge to the Fraser estuary, namely Iona (70 MGD-million gallons per day), Lulu (3 MGD) and Annacis (34 MGD) (Figure 8). Treatment at these plants is primary which means that the settleable particles and up to 30 percent of the biochemical oxygen demand are removed. Prior to the construction of Annacis Island Sewage Treatment Plant there were several direct discharges to the river in the vicinity of Burnaby, New Westminster and Surrey. Most of these have now been intercepted. Further up the Fraser Valley small communities such as Chilliwack, Mission and Maple Ridge have sewage treatment plants which discharge their effluents to the Fraser. Treatment in most cases is secondary followed by chlorination. The secondary treatment removes the settleable

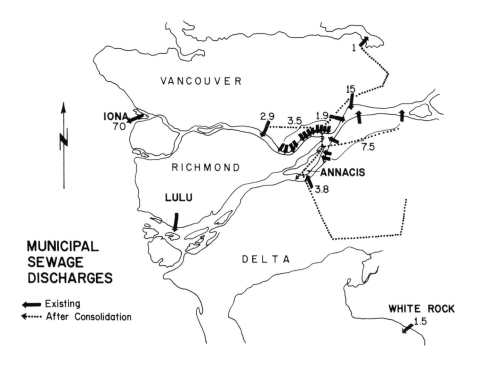

Figure 8   Source: Hall and Koch (1976).

particles and may remove 90 percent of the biochemical oxygen demand. Chlorination is used to kill the pathogens, but even with 99 percent kill, large numbers of viable microorganisms can still be discharged to the river. Also, in the case of plants such as Iona which are combined (i.e. handle urban runoff and sanitary wastes), chlorination does not take place in the fall and winter months when storm runoff is high.

Other sources of pollutants to the Fraser are direct industrial dischargers such as sawmills, fish processing plants and chemical industries. There are as many as 88 industries presently discharging to the Lower Fraser with 80 percent of these discharges below Port Mann Bridge (Table 4). Twelve of these industries have discharges in excess of one million gallons per day. It was not possible in our research to determine the characteristics of these discharges and the only information available from the Pollution Control Branch permits and applications is on flow, biochemical oxygen demand, suspended solids and total dissolved solids. Pollution Control Branch data on such parameters as coliforms and trace metals are either very fragmentary, or below some detection limit which is frequently not low enough. Therefore, no useful information on the significance of direct industrial discharges as contributors of trace metals and coliforms to the lower Fraser is currently available.

TABLE 4

DIRECT INDUSTRIAL DISCHARGES TO
THE LOWER FRASER RIVER

Number of Industries[1]	Discharge (gal/day)
34 (7)	1,000 — 10,000
28 (9)	10,000 — 100,000
14 (0)	100,000 — 1,000,000
12 (1)	> 1,000,000
total 88 (17)	

1. bracketed values indicate number of industries above Port Mann Bridge
Hall and Koch (1976).

Another important source of pollutants is urban runoff from stormwater. Since a large portion of urban runoff reaches the Fraser as overland flow in small streams and storm sewers, it is very difficult to monitor all of these discharges. In addition, the quality of urban runoff is influenced by a number of factors, such as land use, soil and surface characteristics, slope of land, intensity and duration of rainfall, and dry fallout patterns. However, our studies of storm water and combined sewers have provided an indication of the importance of stormwater as a source of trace metals.

Source of Trace Metals

To conduct this study three sewage treatment plants in the Greater Vancouver area (Iona, Lulu and White Rock) and seven sewerage sub-basins, all of which have different land use characteristics were selected. This was done to delineate some of the sources of trace metals. The sites chosen for this study represented a wide range of different wastewater types. For example the Iona sewage treatment plant receives storm runoff and both domestic and industrial sewage, Lulu sewage treatment plant is a sanitary system and in addition to domestic wastes receives a significant contribution (about 4 percent of its wastes), from a metal finishing industry. The White Rock sewage treatment plant is a separate sewerage system receiving mainly domestic wastewaters. The seven sewage sub-basins chosen provided a finer delineation of different contributors. For example one area received only stormwater and another area was strongly influenced by the presence of four metal finishing industries.

The data collected in this study may be summarized by grouping them into three categories: residential wastewater, mixed system wastewaters (includes residential, industrial and commercial components) and mixed system + metal-finishers. Figure 9 shows the overall average and range of average concentrations for four trace metals, namely copper, nickel, lead and zinc in these three categories. The concentration scales for nickel and zinc are logarithmic, that is, they increase by multiples of 10 rather than in a linear fashion. From this figure it is readily apparent that there is an increase in the average concentrations of all four metals as one moves from residential wastes through mixed system wastewaters to those containing electroplating wastes. In residential

Burnaby electroplater. F. Cady

Trace Metals in Sewage

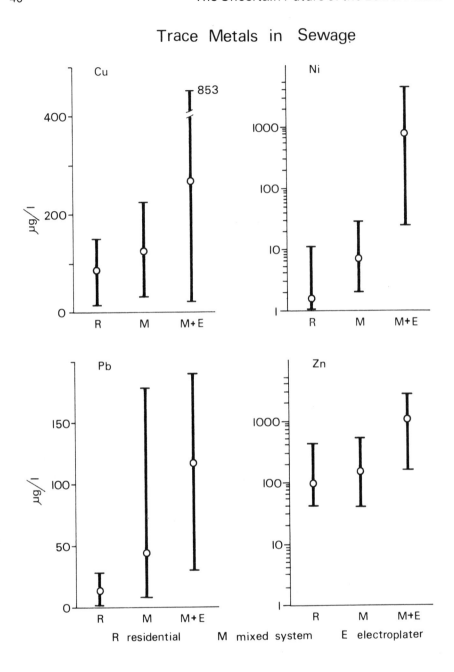

Figure 9   Source: Koch *et al.*, (1976).

discharges, copper and zinc appear to be the most important metals. Where do they enter the residential wastewater system? Analysis of the water supply at various stages in the distribution system indicated that a major portion of the copper and zinc in residential wastewater was attributable to corrosion within our household piping system. This appears to be caused by the high corrosion potential of our water supply which is very soft. Certainly everyone in the Lower Mainland must be aware of the blue deposits on tubs and sinks as a result of a leaking faucet. Where there are industrial and commercial discharges the average trace metal concentration increases, but the most dramatic increase in trace metals takes place when metal finishers discharge to the system. For example, nickel concentrations increase 1000 times and zinc by a factor of 10 when compared to residential values.

What about stormwater effects? During a rainfall, surface runoff transports contaminants which have been deposited on streets into the sewerage system. As a result, lead concentrations increased in all three drainage categories during the wet weather period. Copper and zinc often showed higher concentrations during a rainfall event but changes were much lower than for lead. If the rain continued for an extended period, concentrations of most trace metals usually decreased as they were effectively flushed from the streets and the sewerage system.

The data summarized above are for several sewerage systems taken together. If a single wastestream is studied in detail it will be found that there is considerable variation in trace metal concentrations throughout the day (Figure 10). For example, peak concentrations of copper, nickel, lead and zinc at the White Rock sewage treatment plant usually occur in late morning or early afternoon, coincident with periods of peak flow. Minimum concentrations are coincident with low flows which occur in the early morning. The other treatment plants show similar trends, although the variations are not as distinct due to larger contributions from industrial and commercial areas with more variable discharges which tend to smooth out the extremes. Such variations have important implications with regard to the acute toxicity of sewage and any treatment technology for removal of trace metals at the sewage treatment plant. For example, it may only be necessary to treat the sewage for metal removal during the period of peak trace metal discharge in order to reduce the toxicity to acceptable discharge standards.

This discussion has considered only concentrations of trace metals, but the load of material discharged is an important factor to consider in assessing the impact of the waste discharges. For example, even though residential concentrations of a pollutant may be low the large volume of wastes may make this an important source. Likewise, if the concentration of a certain pollutant is very high, as in the case of electroplating wastes, small volumes of waste can still be important. The latter point may be illustrated by taking as an example the Burnaby South Slope sewer, which has four electroplating industries discharging to it and contributes on a per capita basis 130 times as much nickel and 14 times as much zinc as the Iona sewage treatment plant. A similar comparison between Iona and Lulu sewage treatment plant which gets 4 percent of its waste from a

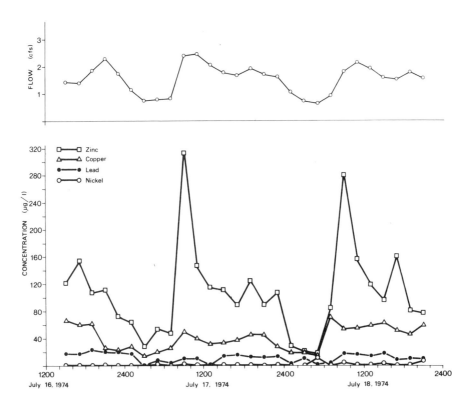

DAILY VARIATION IN TRACE METALS AND
FLOW AT WHITE ROCK TREATMENT PLANT

Figure 10   Source: Koch *et al*, (1976)

metal finisher, indicates that Lulu has a per capita loading 20 times higher for nickel and 8 times higher for cadmium.

The effect of a storm on trace metal loading in the sewerage system is presented in Figure 11 which shows the loading of four metals, namely copper, nickel, lead and zinc at the Iona sewage treatment plant in November. The dry weather load has been subtracted from the total loading during this period so the data presented is attributable solely to the storm and indicates that stormwater is an important source of some trace metals.

With this kind of information, plus population estimates of different areas and rainfall data, it is possible to estimate the residential, non-domestic and stormwater contributions of trace metals to the Lower Fraser. Table 5 shows the contribution of domestic sources, non-domestic sources and surface runoff to the load of copper, nickel, lead and zinc that are discharged to the Lower Fraser from the three sewage treatment plants (Iona, Lulu and Annacis) the Burnaby South Slope sewer (which was not connected to Annacis when sewage quality data was obtained) and urban runoff. Industry discharging directly to the river has not

TRACE METAL LOAD IN STORMWATER

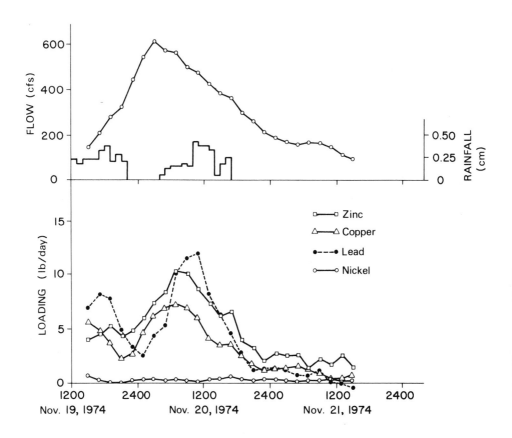

Figure 11   Source: Koch *et al.*, (1976).

TABLE 5

SOURCES OF TRACE METALS TO LOWER FRASER[1]

Area	Copper	Nickel	Lead	Zinc
Domestic Wastes	57	4	10	34
Non-domestic Wastes	30	86	33	51
Urban Runoff	13	10	56	15

1. expressed as percent of measured sources
Hall and Koch (1976).

TABLE 6
SOURCES OF TOTAL COLIFORMS TO LOWER FRASER[1]

Source	No Treatment	Chlorination at STP[2]
Domestic Wastes	37.1	28.5
Non-domestic Wastes	62.6	48.2
Urban Runoff	0.3	23.3

1. expressed as percent of measured sources
2. assuming 99% disinfection
Hall and Koch (1976).

been included as there is inadequate data. Domestic wastes contribute almost 60 percent of the copper from these sources, and as mentioned above, this appears to come from the distribution system. In the case of nickel, 86 percent is attributable to non-domestic wastes with the metal finishing industries one of the major contributors. Over half of the lead (56 percent) comes from urban runoff, which implicates the automobile as one of the major contributors of lead to our waterways. Zinc appears to be contributed by both domestic and non-domestic waste sources with a small contribution from urban runoff. The importance of this type of information is readily apparent in the event that it were decided to control discharges of these trace metals to the Fraser. It shows, for example, that it serves no purpose to try to reduce lead discharges by treatment at the sewage treatment plant, since over half of the lead in the river comes from urban runoff. It would appear that a more effective means of controlling lead would be to eliminate it from gasoline. Similarly nickel should be removed before it gets diluted in the sewers by, for example, a source control programme at the metal finishing industries.

Source of Pathogens

Assuming that the coliform microorganisms are adequate indicators of the presence of pathogens, estimates similar to those made for trace metals can be made to determine the importance of domestic wastes, non-domestic wastes and urban runoff as sources of pathogens. Again it should be stressed that average flows and coliform numbers have been used to arrive at the distribution of coliforms among the different waste sources considered. Table 6 presents the data as a percentage of the measured sources and does not include any data for direct industrial discharge to the river. If there were no disinfection at the sewage treatment plants, almost 40% of the pathogens would be derived from domestic wastewaters with sixty percent from non-domestic sources. However, if chlorination is used to remove 99% of the pathogens the contribution from these two sources drops considerably. With the present system of disinfection, 99% removal is not usually achieved since combined sewerage systems such as Iona do not bother to chlorinate outside of the swimming season. Even if disinfection at all plants was 99 percent and the total numbers of microorganisms reduced, there would still be a large enough contribution from uban runoff to give some high values in the river. Disinfection of this source would be very difficult since it is of a sporadic nature with high numbers usually occurring during a rainfall event.

SUMMARY AND CONCLUSIONS

The information presented in this chapter provides a description of water quality conditions in the Lower Fraser River and sources of the more important pollutants. Even though large amounts of organic wastes are discharged to the Lower Fraser, oxygen conditions are very good, never dropping below 85 percent of the saturation value. The nutrient status of the Lower Fraser is also very good with nitrogen and phosphorus concentrations quite low when compared to other major river systems in North America. There appear to be two main water quality problems in the Lower Fraser both apparently attributable to the urban-industrial complex of metropolitan Vancouver namely, pathogens and trace metals. There are high levels of indicator microorganisms, which suggest the presence of pathogens and limit the safe use of the water. The micro-biological quality of the water deteriorates from being marginally acceptable for drinking water at Hope to being almost unacceptable for any use, even irrigation, in some reaches of the North Arm. Potential problems are apparent regarding toxic substances such as trace metals. Concentrations are not high enough to be acutely toxic to fish but the sporadic occurrence of higher concentrations of trace metals such as lead, mercury and zinc in the lower reaches of the river and accumulations in sediments give some cause for concern especially since these substances are not biodegradable and bioamplification through food chain concentration or direct absorption by the organism cannot be ignored in the sensitive estuarine areas of the Lower Fraser. Although the concentrations of chlorinated hydrocarbons and other toxic substances such as phenols and detergents appear to be low, not enough information is available to assess the importance of these substances in water quality of the Lower Fraser.

Consideration in this chapter has only been given to the sources of trace metals and pathogens. Both of these pollutants appear to originate from very diverse sources. The largest portion of copper comes from domestic wastes and appears to be attributable to corrosion of household piping systems by our water supply which is very soft and has a high corrosion potential. Metal finishing industries are responsible for most of the nickel and almost half of the zinc discharged to the Lower Fraser. Urban runoff is the main source of lead discharged to the aquatic environment implicating the automobile as the main source of this pollutant. Domestic and non-domestic wastes contribute large numbers of pathogens to the Fraser. Large numbers can be removed by disinfection at the sewage treatment plants. However, high numbers of coliforms will probably still occur in some reaches of the river as a result of direct discharge of stormwater and the practice of not disinfecting sewage at Iona sewage treatment plant during the high flow winter period.

REFERENCES

B.C. Research. 1975. *Annacis Island outfall dilution study.* Project 1524. Report no. 4. B.C. Research, Vancouver.

Bourque, S.C. and Adams, E.C.W. 1975. *Environmental impact assessment small craft harbour proposal at Ladner, B.C.* The Corporation of Delta, Delta, B.C.

Buhler, D.R. 1972. Environmental contamination by toxic metals in the environment. In *Heavy metals in the environment.* SEMN WR 016.73. Water Resources Research Institute, Oregon State University, Corvallis.

Federal Water Pollution Control Federation. 1968. *Water quality criteria.* FWPCF, Washington.

Hall, K.J. and Fletcher, K. 1974. Trace metals pollution from a metropolitan area: sources and accumulation in the Lower Fraser estuary. In *Proceedings of the International Conference on Transport of Persistent Chemicals in Aquatic Ecosystems.* 83-87. Ottawa, Canada.

Hall, K.J. and Koch, F.A. 1976. *Waste loadings to the Lower Fraser from sewers, sewage treatment plants and surface runoff.* Westwater Research Centre, University of British Columbia, Vancouver, (in preparation).

Hall, K.J.; Koch, F.A.; and Yesaki, I. 1974. *Further investigations into water quality conditions in the Lower Fraser River system.* Technical Report no. 4. Westwater Research Centre, University of British Columbia, Vancouver.

Johnston, N.T.; Albright, L.J.; Northcote, T.G.; Oloffs, P.C.; and Tsumura, K. 1975. *Chlorinated hydrocarbon residues in fishes from the Lower Fraser River.* Technical Report no. 9. Westwater Research Centre, University of British Columbia, Vancouver.

Joy, C.S. 1975. *Water quality models of the Lower Fraser River.* Technical Report no. 6. Westwater Research Centre, University of British Columbia, Vancouver.

Koch, F.A.; Hall, K.J.; and Yesaki, I. 1976. *Toxic substances in wastewater of a metropolitan area.* Westwater Research Centre, University of British Columbia, Vancouver, (in preparation).

Ward, P.R.B. 1975. *Dispersion of pollutants in a partially stratified estuary.* Westwater Research Centre, University of British Columbia, Vancouver, (in preparation).

Float studies of surface currents.
Fraser North Arm, looking east near Queensborough.

Westwater
Doug Miller

Fraser River near Agassiz   Westwater

Fraser Mills Industrial Complex, New Westminster.   Ken Hall

4

The Quality of Water in Tributaries of the Lower Fraser and Sources of Pollution

by Kenneth J. Hall and John H. Wiens

In this chapter water and sediment quality in the tributaries of the Lower Fraser is summarized and compared with that found in the Fraser. Two case studies are given. The first is a detailed study carried out on the Salmon River to determine the effects of land use and soil characteristics on quality of water in this small rural agricultural, low density residential basin. The second case study presents a discussion of the effects of intense urbanization upon the water and sediment quality of the Still Creek-Brunette River system, looking in detail at the quality of stormwater runoff and sources of contamination.

Three important questions are addressed, namely:

1. What are the water quality conditions in the tributaries and what impact do they have on the Fraser?
2. What are the sources of pollutants of concern and their pathways to the water?
3. How do water quality conditions and sources of pollutants differ in the types of tributary drainage basins we have studied?

WATER QUALITY IN THE TRIBUTARIES

The tributaries which enter the Fraser downstream of Hope add an additional 22 percent (27,500 cfs) to its flow. They can be divided into two groups. The first group flow from forested watersheds which have extensive drainage at higher elevations in the coastal mountains. Their flow regime is controlled by snowmelt at higher elevations, similar to the Fraser. The major tributaries in this group include the Pitt, Stave, Harrison and Chilliwack Rivers, which contribute 94 percent of the flow added to the Fraser below Hope and some minor mountain streams such as the Coquitlam, Norrish and Silverhope (Figure 1). These rivers are aesthetically pleasing and usually appear very clean when compared to the muddy Fraser. The second group of tributaries are the small creeks and rivers which drain the lowlands of the Fraser. Since they are located at lower elevations, their flow is controlled by the seasonal patterns of precipitation. They contribute only one percent of the flow added to the Fraser below Hope. In most cases discharge of these to the Fraser is regulated by control structures to prevent flooding when water levels in the Fraser are high. This can result in stagnant, slow moving waters in the lower reaches of these tributaries. These tributaries include Chilliwack-Atchelitz Creek, and the Sumas and Salmon Rivers which drain mainly agricultural basins, and the Brunette River system which drains part of the urban-industrial complex of metropolitan Vancouver.

LOWER FRASER RIVER AND TRIBUTARIES

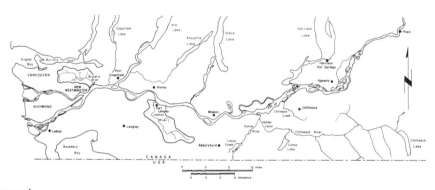

Figure 1

Oxygen, BOD and Nutrients

To facilitate discussion of water quality conditions in the tributaries they are divided into mountain, agricultural and metropolitan drainage basins on the basis of their major land use. Table 1 summarizes average concentrations of dissolved oxygen, BOD and the nutrients, nitrogen and phosphorus, in each category of basin. The complete data and analytical techniques are presented by

TABLE 1

WATER QUALITY IN TRIBUTARIES AND FRASER

River	Oxygen	BOD	Total Nitrogen	Total Phosphorus
Fraser	11.5	2	0.4	0.08
Mountain Trib.	11.5	2	0.1	0.03
Agricultural Trib.	8.7	4	1.0	0.11
Metropolitan Trib.	10.3	3	0.6	0.04

values in parts per million (ppm)
Hall *et al.*, (1974)

Hall *et al.* (1974). The mountain tributaries are all very similar to the mainstem Fraser for oxygen and degradable organic matter. However both the agricultural and metropolitan tributaries show poorer oxygen conditions than in the main river. Chilliwack-Atchelitz Creek has the poorest water quality, with BOD values reaching 11 ppm (parts per million or milligrams per litre) and oxygen concentrations frequently less than 5 ppm. During a preliminary survey in August 1972 anoxic conditions (i.e. - zero dissolved oxygen) were found in Chilliwack-Atchelitz Creek, and dissolved oxygen values of < 1 ppm were measured in the Salmon River in the stagnant waters behind the flow control structures for these two tributaries. Hence, there are areas in the lower reaches of these tributaries where fish could not survive during the warm summer months.

Nitrogen and phosphorus show much lower average concentrations in the mountain tributaries than were found in the Fraser. This difference may be attributable to a lower level of disturbance in these river valleys, resulting in less erosion and leaching of nutrients from the soils. Nutrient concentrations are highest in those tributaries classified as agricultural. The largest difference occurs for nitrogen, with an average value ten times that found in the mountain tributaries. The highest nitrogen values were found in the Salmon River and highest phosphorus concentrations in Chilliwack-Atchelitz Creek. All the tributaries in the Agricultural-Metropolitan group have some nitrogen concentrations which exceed the critical nitrogen level established for lakes. Whether this represents a significant nutrient enrichment problem for a river has not been established. However, all of these tributaries have flow control structures making the lower reaches very characteristic of an impoundment, and algal blooms have been observed in the more stagnant waters during the low summer flows.

Pathogens and Trace Metals

Pathogen indicator microorganisms and trace metal concentrations are summarized in Table 2. The mountain tributaries show numbers of total and fecal coliforms which are 1/10 the average values found in the Lower Fraser

TABLE 2

WATER QUALITY IN TRIBUTARIES AND FRASER

River	Total Coliforms	Fecal Coliforms	Copper	Lead	Mercury	Zinc
Fraser	15,500	4,150	4	<1	<0.05	7
Mountain Tributary	1,716	410	2	<1	<0.05	8
Agricultural Tributary	10,844	539	2	<1	<0.05	5
Metropolitan Tributary	9,986	2,486	7	6	<0.05	16

coliforms in numbers/100 ml
trace metals in ppb
Hall *et al.* (1974)

TABLE 3

ACCEPTABLE TRIBUTARY WATER USE

Water Use	Tributary
Raw drinking water	Harrison River
Recreation	
a. primary contact	Chilliwack R., Deer Cr.
b. recreation other than primary contact	Sumas R., Lonzo Cr., Salmon R., Pitt R., Brunette R.
Irrigation	Chilliwack-Atchelitz Cr.
No acceptable use	Still Cr.

Hall *et al.* (1974)

River. Even those tributaries draining the agricultural and urban areas in the valley do not have average values as high as those for the Fraser; however, some of them are in very poor condition if they are judged on acceptable use based on fecal coliform numbers (Table 3). Lowest numbers are found in the Harrison, which could be used as a drinking water source. Next come the Chilliwack River and Deer Creek, which could be used for contact sports such as swimming. The Sumas, Lonzo, Salmon, Pitt and Brunette Rivers are all safe for recreation other than primary contact, while Chilliwack-Atchelitz Creek is only acceptable for irrigation purposes, and Still Creek is not safe for any use.

Trace metals, as represented by the four elements copper, lead, mercury and zinc, do not show large concentration differences in mountain and agricultural tributaries when compared with average values for the Fraser River. However, the Still Creek-Brunette River system, which represents a metropolitan drainage basin, has higher concentrations of copper, lead and zinc than have been found in the main river. Whereas our analyses conducted in the Fraser, as described in the previous chapter, found no evident differences in the average concentrations between Fraser River stations adjacent to metropolitan Vancouver and those further upstream. Lead shows the largest increase, with average values six times those for the other watersheds. Copper and zinc concentrations are approximately double. Comparison of the toxicity of a combination of these three trace metals indicates that even on the average the tributaries within the metropolitan area, Brunette River and Still Creek, exceed the 'threshold of harm', with concentrations in Still Creek almost twice the level where there could be some effect upon the fish (Figure 2). For each sampling date we find that Still Creek water exceeds the 'threshold of harm' to rainbow trout 82 percent of the sampling times, whereas one of the more contaminated stations on the Fraser, Queensboro Bridge (Figure 7 chapter 3) exceeds this criterion only 43 percent of the time. Also, lead becomes a much more significant contributor to the trace metal toxicity of the water in the metropolitan drainage basin.

SEASONAL VARIATION IN TOXICITY

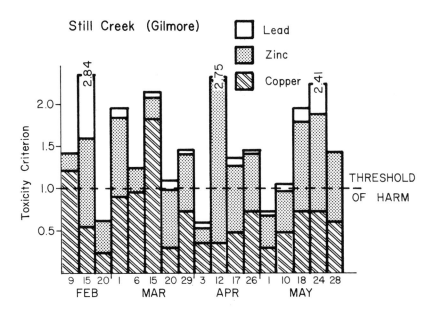

Figure 2   Source: Hall *et al.*, (1974).

TABLE 4

TOXIC SUBSTANCES IN SEDIMENTS

River	Copper	Lead	Zinc	DDT	PCB's
Fraser	10 - 100	5 - 12	25 - 60	—	—
Mountain Tributary	10 - 50	7 - 12	17 - 85	—	—
Agricultural Tributary	12 - 32	1 - 35	48 - 129	<1 - 4	<1 - 52
Metropolitan Tributary	11 - 1765	4 - 950	32 - 990	<4 - 189	<10 - 780

trace metals in ppm
chlorinated hydrocarbons in ppb
Benedict *et al.* (1973); Hall *et al.* (1976a) and Hall *et al.* (1976b).

Toxic Substances in Sediments

As was pointed out in the previous chapter, sediments are important in water quality studies, as they tend to accumulate the insoluble pollutants such as trace metals and chlorinated hydrocarbons which are discharged to our waterways. Table 4 summarizes the range of selected trace metals, (copper, lead and zinc) and the chlorinated hydrocarbons (DDT and PCB's) found in tributary sediments and compares them with Fraser River sediments (Table 4). Very little difference is evident between copper, lead and zinc in sediments of the Fraser and mountain tributaries. The agricultural tributaries show some higher concentrations of lead (3x) and zinc (2x) than found in the Fraser, while the metropolitan tributaries show the largest differences, with concentrations for all three trace metals often ten times greater than the maximum value found in the Fraser. Chlorinated hydrocarbons were only measured in the agricultural and metropolitan tributaries, but again concentrations of both DDT and polychlorinated biphenyls were much higher in the metropolitan watershed. Also, the frequency of detection of these chlorinated compounds was much greater in the Brunette basin. Out of 37 samples analyzed in the Salmon and Sumas River basin, only one contained detectable DDT and eight contained measurable concentrations of PCB's. On the other hand, in the thirty sediment samples from the Brunette, more than one third of them contained DDT and over 50 percent contained polychlorinated biphenyls. In addition to these chlorinated hydrocarbons, α and γ chlordanes were found at four stations in a reach of Still Creek. The locations of these contaminated areas and possible sources of these pollutants are discussed in the latter part of this paper.

Sampling Site in the Brunette River.   Westwater

WATER QUALITY AND POLLUTANT SOURCES IN
A RURAL-AGRICULTURAL BASIN

Let us now look at water quality conditions in a rural-agricultural basin — the Salmon — and consider some of the sources and pathways of the pollutants that enter the stream. It will be seen that although the sources are non-point or diffuse and hence difficult to identify, water quality conditions appear nevertheless to be related more closely to urbanization than to agricultural activities.

Hydrology and Land Use

In urban basins man has altered and added to the routes of movement of water and, therefore, the transport of pollutants. On the one hand, supply and distribution systems have added large volumes of water that are additional to precipitation to the basin. Some of this water is used consumptively, but much of it is used simply to transport domestic or industrial wastes. On the other hand, storm and sanitary sewer systems, in combination with roof areas, surfaced streets and parking lots have reduced greatly the amount and proportion of precipitation water entering ground and surface water in ways normal to the hydrologic cycle. In effect then, these alterations short circuit natural routes. Water does not infiltrate into and leach through the soil to groundwater and thence to surface waters. As a result, pollutants reaching these impermeable surface areas, as, for example, by fallout, are moved relatively more quickly and directly to the water environment.

In rural basins, normal routes of the hydrologic cycle still carry the largest portion of incoming water. Figure 3 depicts the movement of water through an ecosystem. Precipitation falling on the earth's surface moves downslope over the land surface or infiltrates the soil, and moves to streams or other surface water bodies by subsurface or groundwater flow. Ultimately water again enters the atmosphere by evaporation from the surface or by transpiration from plants. Water then is a key component of the environment, linking the atmosphere, vegetation, soil, and stream components of the system. Water acts as a carrier of materials as well as energy between the atmosphere, land, and the stream. Examples of the carrier function of water are the erosion and transport to streams of sediment and the leaching of nutrient elements through the soil to the stream. It is therefore necessary to understand hydrologic processes in order to understand the processes which affect water quality in streams.

Even in rural basins man's activities influence water quantity and quality. Drainage ditches, canals, floodgates, dams and pumps have been added to influence flow for his benefit. Land use activities may increase amounts of water entering the system, for example by irrigation or by subsurface sewage disposal. Alteration of the land in any way affects the condition of the land surface and therefore its runoff and infiltration characteristics. Also additions to the soil of fertilizers, pesticides, animal manures or perhaps urban wastes, affect the materials available for leaching or runoff to streams.

THE HYDROLOGIC CYCLE

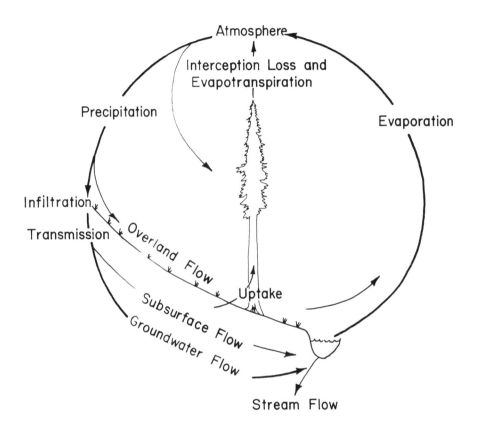

Figure 3   Source: Brown (1974).

The Salmon River Watershed

The Salmon River enters the Fraser River at Fort Langley (Figure 1). Its flow regime is controlled by seasonal precipitation patterns and therefore the hydrograph shows a distinct low flow period from June to October and a high flow period from November to April or May (Figure 4). Its drainage basin is about 32 square miles in area and has a variety of soils, some on Fraser River alluvium, some on sandy and gravelly glacial outwash, some on marine clays, and some on stony or clayey glacio-marine materials. The nature of these materials influences stream flow, distribution of land use activities, water chemistry and stream bed material characteristics. All of these in turn directly or indirectly affect stream bed organisms and fish habitat.

The Salmon River serves as habitat for a number of fresh water and migratory fish species, most notably coho salmon, cutthroat and steelhead trout. (McMynn and Vernon, 1954; Hartman, 1968; Hartman and Gill, 1968). Concern for and

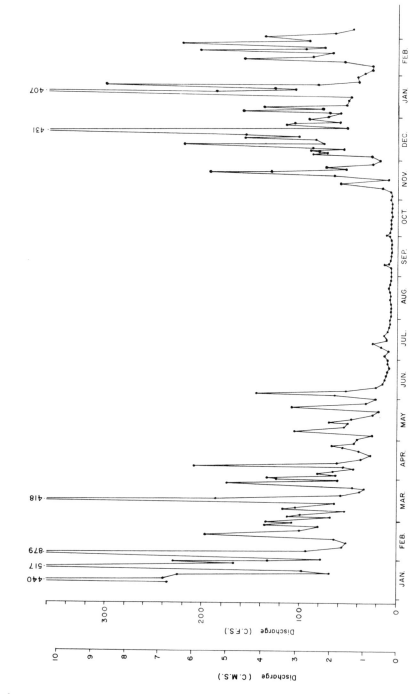

DISCHARGE PATTERN IN THE SALMON RIVER

Figure 4

Source: Wiens and Beale (1976).

enhancement of habitat for fish on the Salmon River must be considered. In the upper and middle reaches the stream has varied characteristics from slough-like conditions with little if any water during the summer, to that of a pleasant, clear, shaded, forest-stream. In the lower reaches, on the other hand, the grade is low, flow is sluggish and the river appears somewhat muddy.

In such a rural-agricultural basin it is particularly difficult to attribute measured stream water quality conditions at a point to land use and soil conditions on the land. Sources for the most part are diffuse and non-point. There are no effluent sewer pipes to sample. Somewhat indirect approaches must be used and inferences made.

The Study Procedure

In our study of the Salmon River, sampling points were identified on the river, critical with respect to land use and soil conditions. Maps were prepared depicting land use, soil parent materials, soil drainage and slope (Slaymaker and Lavkulich, 1976). In transparent form these maps were overlaid and the points

The Salmon River near Langley, B.C. is typical of the Lower Mainland agricultural tributaries.   John Wiens

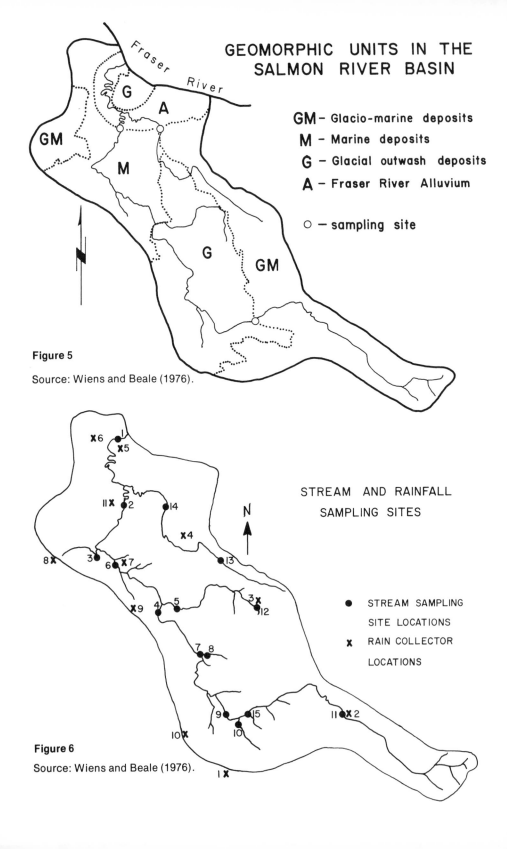

GEOMORPHIC UNITS IN THE
SALMON RIVER BASIN

Fraser River

G
A
GM
M
G
GM

GM – Glacio-marine deposits
M – Marine deposits
G – Glacial outwash deposits
A – Fraser River Alluvium

○ – sampling site

N

Figure 5

Source: Wiens and Beale (1976).

STREAM AND RAINFALL
SAMPLING SITES

N

● STREAM SAMPLING
SITE LOCATIONS

X RAIN COLLECTOR
LOCATIONS

Figure 6

Source: Wiens and Beale (1976).

representing significant changes in soils and land use chosen. Figure 5 shows in a simplified form how sampling points on the river were chosen. Subdivisions of the landscape were made which we called geomorphic units. At points on the river where transition from one to another occurred, a station was established. Land use patterns were taken into account in a similar manner.

Fourteen stations (Figure 6) were established in this way, and from the late spring of 1974 until the spring of 1975 water was sampled and analysed for general chemical and physical parameters, oxygen, organic carbon, nutrients, major ions and trace metals. Earlier analysis of water samples for chlorinated hydrocarbons had not detected any (Hall *et al.*, 1974) and so sampling of stream bed sediments was therefore carried out both before and after the pesticide use season.

Water Quality Conditions of the Salmon River and Pollution Sources

Relative to forested streams, rural-agricultural streams are poorer in quality with respect to some parameters, but conditions are still generally good.

In the following paragraphs some water quality conditions in the Salmon will be discussed. Reference will be made to sources responsible for poorer conditions to the extent they could be determined. In particular, oxygen, nitrates, heavy metals and chlorinated hydrocarbons will be emphasized. It will be seen that with respect to nitrates and trace metals particularly, interactions of soil properties with land use activities are important in explaining some water quality conditions.

Temperature

Firstly, a word about water temperatures. Temperature conditions of the stream affect water suitability as habitat and the growth rates of fish (Hartman, 1968). Man-made changes such as stream bank vegetation removal or flow control can affect temperature markedly. In this study, measured temperature conditions of the Salmon River showed a very favourable picture (Table 5). Most mean summer temperatures were in a range suitable for good growth rates of coho and trout. Except for the lower reach stations where water is exposed and subject to higher temperatures, flow and stream bank alterations potentially detrimental to temperature conditions have not occurred.

Oxygen and Organic Carbon

Agricultural land use activities are a potential source of degradable, oxygen demanding substances. Erosion of soil organic matter, runoff of farmyard wastes and animal manures applied to the land, or perhaps even direct entry of animals into streams are potential sources and can result in BOD loads and reduced dissolved oxygen. In this study oxygen levels were generally very good, being in the range of 10-11 mg/l and near saturation (Table 6). Two points of significance are worth making. At a sampling station at the outflow of an impounded farm pond, mean dissolved oxygen levels during the summer months were 5.3 mg/l, below the 6.0 mg/l suggested as critical to extended trout survival. Flow was very low, however, so overall effects to the river were considered minor. Secondly, high organic carbon values were generally recorded at the onset of the fall rains and increased flow. This was associated with high suspended sediment values and indicates movement of organic materials as eroding sediments.

TABLE 5

MEAN HIGH AND LOW-FLOW VALUES FOR
TEMPERATURE OF THE SALMON RIVER

Station No.	Temperature	
	Low Flow	High Flow
1	12.0°C	5.0°C
2	10.9	5.0
3	11.8	5.0
4	9.5	6.7
5	8.8	7.3
6	10.2	6.7
7	9.8	7.3
8	8.7	7.3
9	9.8	5.0
10	11.2	6.0
11	6.7	4.0
12	6.3	2.5
14	10.0	5.0
15	10.7	6.3

Wiens and Beale (1976).

Nutrients

Nitrogen and phosphorus, the nutrients of concern as causes of eutrophication were of particular interest in this study. Agricultural use of fertilizers is often believed in large measure to be responsible for eutrophication. It should be noted that we are dealing here with a flowing water ecosystem. The significance of nutrients and especially the critical levels in such a system are largely unknown. The lower part of the Salmon does have a very low grade, and this, in conjunction with flood gates, results in periodic conditions similar to those of a lake or reservoir. As mentioned earlier in this paper, under such conditions algal blooms have been known to occur.

All nitrate levels in the Salmon River were below suggested drinking water limits and well below levels critical to livestock. Levels were all above a suggested level of 0.3 mg/l nitrate critical to excessive growth of algae in lakes (Table 6). Levels were also higher than levels in the mainstem Fraser.

TABLE 6

MEAN HIGH AND LOW-FLOW VALUES FOR OXYGEN, ORGANIC AND NUTRIENT WATER QUALITY PARAMETERS FOR THE SALMON RIVER, LANGLEY, B.C. (mg/l)

Parameter	STATION NUMBER													
	1	2	3	4	5	6	7	8	9	10	11	12	14	15
Dissolved Oxygen	11.23*	11.13	12.27	12.13	11.07	12.77	11.93	12.73	12.63	12.07	13.20	12.90	12.60	11.80
	9.70#	8.44	7.49	11.47	11.30	11.02	10.27	11.12	9.69	5.30	11.65	10.10	10.71	6.09
Total Organic C	4.73	4.13	4.87	3.33	3.53	2.10	6.77	2.93	4.70	4.80	3.70	8.80	4.57	3.57
	5.35	5.87	7.65	7.37	4.27	5.73	5.04	7.05	6.27	6.39	6.80	15.08	5.04	7.61
Total Kjeldahl N	0.23	1.53	0.28	0.29	0.34	0.32	0.38	0.56	0.43	0.43	0.12	0.41	0.36	0.53
	0.35	0.73	1.97	0.92	0.91	1.00	0.70	2.41	1.27	1.62	0.58	0.98	0.82	0.73
Nitrate—N	1.53	1.53	1.50	1.63	1.83	1.67	2.00	2.83	1.35	3.00	1.25	0.80	1.10	1.53
	2.16	3.24	1.72	3.99	4.10	3.75	3.55	5.12	1.26	1.98	1.70	2.38	1.58	1.30
Total P	0.110	0.130	0.070	0.070	0.043	0.097	0.067	0.140	0.317	0.083	0.040	0.100	0.080	0.113
	0.053	0.068	0.089	0.077	0.063	0.068	0.184	0.158	0.086	0.100	0.053	0.158	0.073	0.072

*for high flow (3 sampling dates)
#for low flow (12 sampling dates)
Wiens and Beale (1976)

What about the sources of nitrate? Are agricultural cropping and land fertilization contributing factors? Evidence from stream sampling and map overlaying shows that highest nitrate levels are associated most closely with areas of low density residential developments in the basin and not areas of highest intensity cropping. Correlation analysis between relative areas of this land use and nitrate levels in stream waters gives highest positive values. Furthermore, this situation is particularly apparent in areas where soils are developed on glacial outwash deposits, gravelly and sandy materials. It is believed that septic tank systems (Figure 7) are allowing the leaching of some nitrates to the groundwater and then to the stream. So it does appear that even in rural areas urban influences are contributing significantly to water quality. Normal agricultural field practices cannot be singled out as being responsible for nutrient enrichment in the Salmon River basin.

The contribution to stream nitrate levels from high density poultry production cannot be ruled out. Sampling points associated with areas of such operations also showed higher nitrate values. This is not believed to be necessarily due to land spreading of wastes, but perhaps rather to storage of wastes near the stream bank.

A further point of interest with respect to nitrate is the possible influence of non-commercial forest land, specifically areas of alder immediately adjacent to streams. Alder has a nitrogen fixing capacity. A symbiotic relationship between alder roots and particular micro-organisms facilitates fixation of nitrogen from the air. Some elevated nitrate levels, though certainly not critical levels, appear to be associated with streambank alder. Presumably through nutrient cycling and leaching, some nitrate is reaching surface water from this source.

A SEPTIC TANK – DRAINFIELD SYSTEM

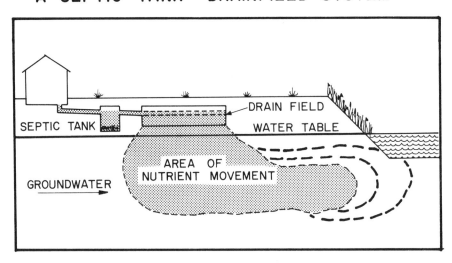

Figure 7   Source: Ellis and Childs (1973).

Phosphorus levels in the water are at or near background levels. In accordance with results of other workers, higher levels were associated with higher flow conditions. This supports the belief that the dominant pathway of phosphorus to streams is by way of attachment to sediments rather than leaching. Sediments are more likely to be entering the stream by bank sloughing during high flow than by overland flow.

Trace Metals

Trace metals are of major environmental concern. Levels in the Fraser mainstem and tributaries have been referred to in the last chapter and earlier in this paper. Agriculture is not believed to be a major source of trace metals in water. To what extent then is the Salmon River affected by trace metals and what are the sources?

If we consider the five trace metals, lead, zinc, copper, nickel and chromium, we can say immediately that lead, nickel and chromium are at very low levels (Table 7). They are near the detection limits of our instruments. Interstation differences are not significant and therefore no inferences about sources can be made.

Measured levels of copper and zinc are more significant. Mean concentrations for high flow and low flow conditions for all fourteen stations on the Salmon River were calculated. The combined toxic contribution relative to a toxicity criterion was then plotted (Inland Waters Branch, 1972). It is apparent from Figure 8 that mean high flow concentrations are more critical than low flow concentrations. Eight of fourteen stations had concentrations which exceeded the threshold of harm suggested for salmonid fishes. In contrast, only two stations under low flow conditions exceeded the threshold. It is therefore suggested that the load at high flow is most significant and that the sources are diffuse rather than point, since dilution with increased flow would be expected if the latter were the case.

The bars in this figure have not been separated into components for copper and zinc. Without exception, however, copper contributed more significantly than zinc.

By looking at the individual station values some broad inferences about sources can be made.

Firstly, station three is seen to have high values for both high and low flow. Of greatest significance in the area contributing runoff to this station is not a particular land use activity, but rather the high proportion of soils of marine sediment origin. Apparently these types of sediments are contributing in some way to levels of these metals in runoff waters. Likewise stations eleven, twelve and fourteen are similarily influenced.

Secondly, stations five and seven and particularly eight have high combined toxicity values. These stations all have high proportions of low density residential land in the areas contributing runoff to them. In addition there is considerable

TABLE 7

MEAN HIGH AND LOW-FLOW VALUES FOR TRACE METALS IN THE SALMON RIVER, LANGLEY, B.C. (mg/l)

Parameter		1	2	3	4	5	6	7	8	9	10	11	12	14	15
									STATION NUMBER							
Iron	a	0.413	0.223	0.283	0.183	0.127	0.283	0.183	0.100	0.250	0.133	0.050	0.100	0.200	0.200
	b	0.333	0.207	0.874	0.083	0.096	0.106	0.110	0.117	0.524	0.751	0.133	0.253	0.247	0.600
Aluminum	a	0.367	0.167	0.357	0.067	0.100	0.100	0.100	0.167	0.133	0.033	0.150	0.150	0.100	0.100
	b	0.075	0.075	0.283	0.0	0.008	0.017	0.017	0.008	0.017	0.030	0.067	0.075	0.043	0.050
Manganese	a	0.010	0.017	0.020	0.003	0.020	0.013	0.030	0.080	0.003	0.013	0.015	0.015	0.017	0.000
	b	0.018	0.271	0.041	0.004	0.003	0.003	0.035	0.118	0.024	0.239	0.013	0.0	0.009	0.030
Silicon	a	4.33	3.33	3.67	2.33	3.33	3.33	2.67	4.33	2.00	2.67	2.00	0.50	3.67	1.35
	b	5.58	5.75	7.08	5.42	6.67	6.33	4.50	6.08	3.17	2.60	1.67	1.75	6.75	3.75
Lead	c	0.0030	0.0004	0.0	0.0	0.0006	0.0009	0.0006	0.0006	0.0	0.0009	0.0015	0.0	0.0006	0.0000
	d	0.0	0.0	0.0	0.0	0.0006	0.0	0.0	0.0	0.0	0.0	0.0	0.0	0.0	0.0000
Zinc	c	0.0033	0.0034	0.0051	0.0019	0.0046	0.0035	0.0030	0.0135	0.0017	0.0020	0.0015	0.0040	0.0009	0.0000
	d	0.0017	0.0025	0.0030	0.0010	0.0035	0.0017	0.0035	0.0058	0.0010	0.0	0.0017	0.0038	0.0	0.0000
Copper	c	0.0036	0.0037	0.0074	0.0044	0.0047	0.0027	0.0042	0.0083	0.0020	0.0064	0.0056	0.0062	0.0036	0.0000
	d	0.0051	0.0030	0.0115	0.0046	0.0036	0.0035	0.0038	0.0025	0.0030	0.0054	0.0039	0.0047	0.0120	0.0000
Nickel	c	0.0015	0.0007	0.0020	0.0005	0.0005	0.0006	0.0005	0.0072	0.0005	0.0004	0.0012	0.0007	0.0012	0.0000
	d	0.0007	0.0007	0.0007	0.0003	0.0003	0.0003	0.0007	0.0	0.0	0.0	0.0	0.0001	0.0	0.0000
Chromium	c	0.0018	0.0018	0.0021	0.0007	0.0009	0.0010	0.0008	0.0061	0.0006	0.0006	0.0010	0.0007	0.0015	0.0000
	d	0.0013	0.0012	0.0017	0.0011	0.0011	0.0014	0.0010	0.0012	0.0004	0.0005	0.0006	0.0003	0.0016	0.0000

a - for high flow (3 sampling times, June '74 - March '75)
b - for low flow (12 sampling times, June '74 - March '75)
c - for high flow (2 sampling times, Dec. 30, '74 - March '75)
d - for low flow (1 sampling time, Jan. 30, '75)
Wiens and Beale (1976)

TRACE METAL TOXICITY INDEX
FOR SALMON RIVER STATIONS

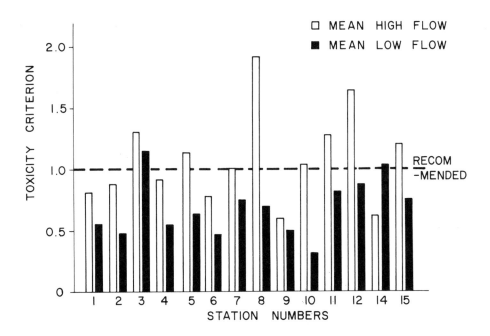

Figure 8   Source: Wiens and Beale (1976).

intensity of poultry production in the vicinity of Station 8. Trace elements, and particularly copper levels here may be due to output from household plumbing systems, although this is not very likely since precipitation or absorption of copper would be expected before entry into stream water. Flushing into streams of poultry wastes, some of which would contain small amounts of trace metals, might be another source. Finally, of course, someone may at some time have dumped copper wire or plumbing scrap into the stream bed.

Chlorinated Hydrocarbons

Bed sediment sampling and analysis for chlorinated hydrocarbons was mentioned earlier. For the Salmon River, only one sample out of fourteen had a very small amount of detectable DDT in the sampling prior to the field season. No station had detectable chlorinated hydrocarbons in August during or after the expected period of greatest pesticide use. (It may be appropriate to comment here that when sampling in the Sumas River, also considered rural-agricultural, the only chlorinated hydrocarbon detected was polychlorinated biphenyl (PCB-Arclor 1254) and this at a stream point probably significantly affected by drainage from the city of Abbotsford rather than agricultural drainage.)

SOURCES OF POLLUTANTS IN AN
URBAN-INDUSTRIALIZED BASIN

The Brunette River-Still Creek system is the only drainage basin in the Lower Fraser Valley completely within the urban-industrial complex of metropolitan Vancouver (Figure 1). It was selected for intensive study to provide a more detailed understanding of the sources of pollutants in urban runoff and the importance of various land use activities in generating these contaminants. The details of this study are presented by Hall *et al.*, (1976a).

The basin contains 15,000 acres and is located within the municipalities of Burnaby, Vancouver, and New Westminster. The main water components of the basin are Still Creek, Deer Lake, Deer Creek, Burnaby Lake and the Brunette River (Figure 9). The Brunette discharges to the mainstem of the Fraser just above Pattullo Bridge at New Westminster. Burnaby mountain on the north side of the basin has an elevation of 1200 feet and is the source of several small fast flowing streams. The basin contains a variety of land uses ranging from parks and open space to intense commercial and industrial development. The basin also serves as a major transportation corridor. Approximately 15 percent of its area is taken up by streets, roads and alleys, making transportation a major land use in the area.

Since storm sewers and sanitary sewers are separate throughout most of the Brunette basin, runoff from the streets is collected by storm sewers and discharged along with natural surface runoff into the various channels of Still Creek and the Brunette River. Still Creek is classified as a storm sewer by the

Looking east toward Burnaby Lake. Highway 401 in foreground.   Westwater

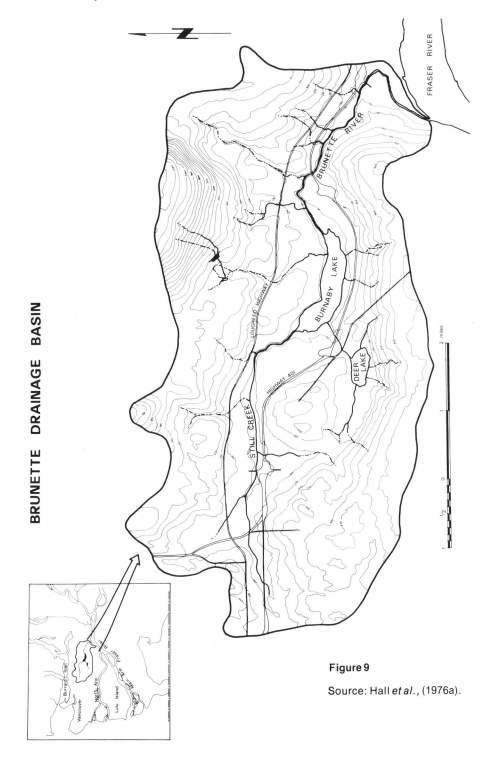

Figure 9

Source: Hall *et al.*, (1976a).

GVSDD (Greater Vancouver Sewage and Drainage District) and several stretches have been channelized and covered. There are a number of illegal sanitary and industrial connections to the storm sewers and some direct industrial discharges are evident in the lower reaches of the Brunette River.

Since the water quality problems in the mainstem Fraser appear to be attributable to the presence of pathogens and toxic substances, only the sources of these quality parameters in the overland drainage of this river basin are discussed in this section.

Trace Metals and Pathogen Indicators in Surface Runoff

Water samples were collected from several stations along Still Creek to assess the importance of a rainfall event in transporting trace metals. At most stations there was an increase in the concentration of copper, lead and zinc under high flow conditions. Lead showed an average increase of 12 times at the six stations in Still Creek (Figure 10). Zinc concentrations increased 2 - 3 times and the average copper concentration doubled under high flow conditions. The importance of a rainfall event is even more significant if flow differences are considered and the load of material estimated. For example at one station on Still Creek, if the flow and concentration during the rainfall event were maintained for one hour, 290 times as much lead would be transported down Still Creek as during an equivalent low flow period.

TRACE METALS IN URBAN RUNOFF

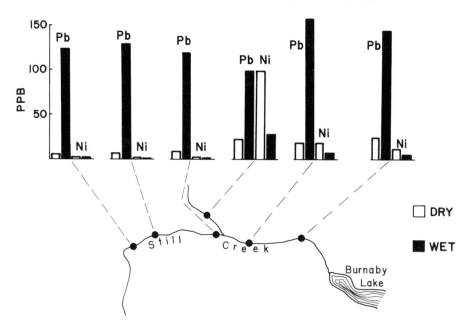

Figure 10   Source: Hall *et al.*, (1976a).

Still Creek entrance to Burnaby Lake

Westwater

Still Creek near Gilmore Road.

Westwater

Urban run-off is a major source of toxic materials   F. Cady

The data presented in Figure 10 also shows the effects of illegal connections to the storm sewer system. In the case of nickel, the concentrations in storm water are usually less than one part per billion as indicated by no change in the nickel concentration under low or high flow conditions for the first three stations. However, once station 3 is passed nickel concentrations increase and are higher during the low flow period than during wet weather conditions. This indicates a direct discharge to be the source of nickel, since there is an apparent dilution during a rainfall event. Such a direct discharge with high nickel, chromium and zinc concentrations was found by GVSDD to be attributable to two electroplaters in Burnaby who were discharging plating waste to the storm sewers. Measures have been taken to correct this problem.

Stormwater can contain high numbers of fecal coliforms from animal wastes. Although the public health significance of these organisms in urban runoff requires more study and evaluation, some research has indicated the presence of pathogens such as *Salmonella* in stormwater with high fecal coliform counts (Geldreich, 1972). As long as the fecal coliform test is used as a measure of the microbiological quality of water, high numbers in stormwater cannot be disregarded as unimportant. Figure 11 shows the concentrations of fecal coliforms in urban runoff in Still Creek (GVSDD, 1974). In an area with no sanitary sewer contamination, numbers averaged less than 1000 organisms/100 mls under dry conditions when most flow is due to groundwater infiltration. However, during rainfall periods these increased to over 4000 organisms/100 mls. Where there was an apparent cross connection between storm and sanitary

FECAL COLIFORMS IN
URBAN RUNOFF

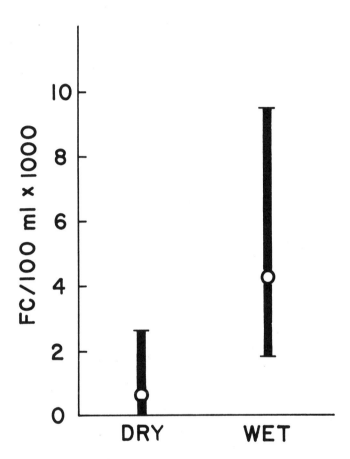

Figure 11   Source: Greater Vancouver Sewerage and Drainage District (1974).

sewers numbers increase very significantly and dry weather values (28,000/100 ml) are almost twice as large as wet weather numbers. Hence, as with nickel, there is a dilution of this direct discharge during the wet weather.

Toxic Substances in Stream Sediments

Since most toxic substances are very insoluble in water they precipitate readily or adsorb to particulate materials and are either transported in the suspended load or settle out and accumulate in the sediments. As a result, sediments tend to present an integrated history of the generation of these materials and their distribution in a drainage basin. Although one cannot often define the exact

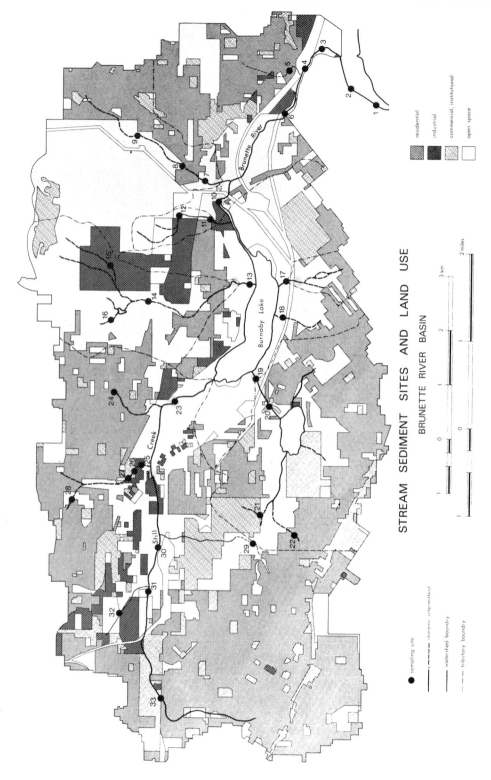

STREAM SEDIMENT SITES AND LAND USE
BRUNETTE RIVER BASIN

residential
industrial
commercial, institutional
open space

sampling site
streams intermittent
watershed boundary
tributary boundary

Figure 12

Source: Hall *et al.*, (1976).

source of a pollutant found in the sediment, this information is very useful in helping to define source areas and allows one to begin to establish causal relationships between land use, traffic density and other important parameters. With this objective in mind surface sediment samples were collected for trace metal and chlorinated hydrocarbon analyses.

Figure 12 shows the distribution of sampling sites in the basin and their relationship to land use. After the samples were analyzed, the data were plotted on an outline of the drainage basin to show the trace metal distribution (Figure 13). From this figure it is apparent from the larger circles that there are accumulations of copper, especially in the lower reaches of Still Creek and in the lower reaches of the Brunette River. Concentrations of copper in the small streams flowing from Burnaby Mountain are very low (less than 20 parts per million). Maps have been constructed for the elements cadmium, cobalt, chromium, iron, mercury, manganese, nickel, lead and zinc and many of them have similar distribution patterns (Hall *et al.*, 1976).

Many of these trace metals occur naturally in our soils and sediments. At what levels are natural background conditions exceeded and an area is considered to be contaminated? Based on more extensive trace metal data from the Lower Fraser Valley an average 'natural' level was determined and an assumption made that everything more than two standard deviations above this level would represent contamination — a rather conservative assumption. On this basis it was found that copper, lead and zinc were the most significant contaminants in the Brunette sediments exceeding this 'natural' level 22, 45, and 25 percent of the time respectively. The reach of Still Creek between Gilmore Avenue (Station 31) and Douglas Road (Station 35) was the area most contaminated with these three trace metals.

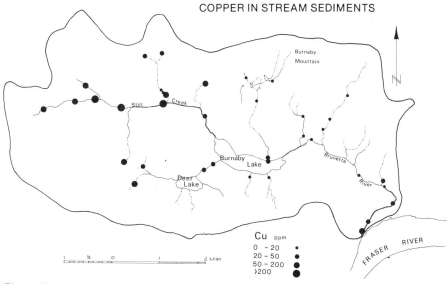

COPPER IN STREAM SEDIMENTS

Cu	ppm	
0 - 20		•
20 - 50		•
50 - 200		●
)200		●

Figure 13

Source: Hall *et al.*, (1976a).

What is the effect of land use upon the trace metal content of the stream sediments? In Table 8, trace metals have been divided into two groups based on land use classification, namely industrial and residential plus greenspace. From this table it is apparent that there are much higher average concentrations of chromium, copper, mercury, nickel, lead and zinc in those sediments collected adjacent to industrial areas. Cadmium, cobalt, iron and manganese do not show large differences between these two land use classifications. This information provides an interesting comparison, and implicates industry as a main contributor of some trace metals found in the sediments. However, it should be kept in mind that the entire drainage area above a sampling site can have an impact upon the trace metal concentration at that point. Also, the flow characteristics of the stream can determine where these materials accumulate. As can be seen from Figure 14, the gradient decreases in the two reaches where most of the higher trace metal concentrations were found. Thus the slower flow and resultant sedimentation in these reaches could be one of the main factors affecting the trace metal distribution in the drainage basin.

Sediment samples were analyzed for fourteen pesticides and polychlorinated biphenyls. The only pesticides found in any of the sediments were DDT, its degradation products DDE and DDD, $\propto$ -chlordane and γ -chlordane. Polychlorinated biphenyls (PCB's) were the most prominent contaminants in this urban-industrial drainage basin with concentrations as high as 780 ppb. Still Creek was very highly contaminated with PCB's. Almost every Still Creek sample contained this chlorinated hydrocarbon with peak concentrations occurring between Willingdon (Station 30) and Gilmore Avenues (Station 31). The chlordanes were found in the same area. The other pesticide, namely DDT and its degradation products, appears to be more scattered throughout the drainage basin. Detectable amounts were measured in some sections which drain residential areas, but the highest values were again detected in the area of Gilmore and Willingdon Avenues where there is extensive industrial land use.

It is difficult to find the exact sources of these contaminants. The use of DDT without a permit has been illegal for several years. However some households and possibly golf courses could have leftover supplies which they are trying to use up; or residuals from past contamination could still be present. Along Still

TABLE 8

TRACE METALS IN STREAM SEDIMENTS AND ADJACENT LAND USE

Land Use	Cd	Co	Cr	Cu	Fe	Hg	Mn	Ni	Pb	Zn
Industrial	0.7	10	122	393	24,000	42	289	29	415	181
Residential & Green Space	< 0.1	7	61	15	21,000	15	308	9	26	50

Values in ppm, except mercury in ppb

Hall *et al.* (1976a)

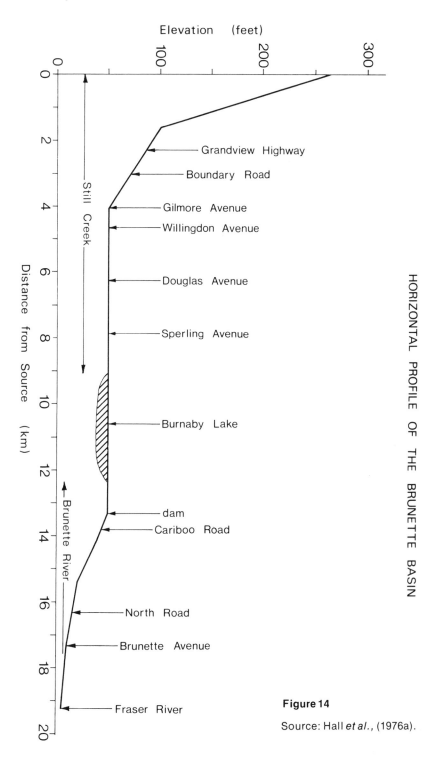

Figure 14

Source: Hall *et al.*, (1976a).

Creek, there are several industries which could contribute PCB's to the environment, although no direct discharges were evident. Since PCB's are used as plasticizers, electrical insulating fluids and as additives to paint, oil and rubber they could originate from many sources (Gustafson, 1970). PCB's have great thermal stability, so combustion of materials containing them results in atmospheric contamination which can ultimately end up in the aquatic environment. In recent year, the sale of PCB's has been limited to uses in enclosed electrical systems, but since they are very persistent substances they will probably be found as environmental contaminants for many years.

Toxic Substances on Street Surfaces

A large percentage of the Brunette basin consists of streets which collect contaminants from atmospheric fallout and other local activities. During periods of rainfall the streets direct runoff to the storm sewers and creeks, thereby transporting the dirt that collects in the streets to the aquatic environment.

To investigate this source of toxic pollutants, street sediment samples were collected from four major land use areas (industrial, commercial, residential and greenspace) and analyzed for eleven trace metals. The more toxic trace metals found on the streets of the different land use areas are summarized in Table 9. Although there was considerable variability in the trace metals found in any one land use area, this table indicates several general trends. By far the largest concentration of copper was associated with industrial areas. Commercial areas, such as large shopping plaza parking lots, contained the highest average concentrations of cadmium, mercury, lead and zinc. As expected, green space areas such as cemetaries and parks contained the lowest concentrations of all trace metals.

Street surface sediments were also analysed for chlorinated hydrocarbons. The same chlorinated hydrocarbons that were found in the stream sediments, namely DDT, its degradation products DDD and DDE, $\propto$ and γ -chlordane and polychlorinated biphenyls were also found on the streets. Although concentrations did not reach the levels that occurred in the sediments of Still Creek they

TABLE 9

TRACE METALS IN STREET SEDIMENTS

Land Use	Cadmium	Copper	Mercury	Nickel	Lead	Zinc
Industrial	1.5	780	60	44	1,240	300
Commercial	2.4	210	120	34	1,415	700
Residential	1.2	130	40	46	710	400
Green Space	1.2	120	20	27	100	250

all values in ppm, except mercury in ppb
Hall *et al.* (1976a)

TABLE 10

CHLORINATED HYDROCARBONS IN STREET SEDIMENTS

Land Use	DDT	PCB
INDUSTRIAL	5	96
COMMERCIAL	8	141
RESIDENTIAL	18	91
GREEN SPACE	15	50

values in parts per billion (ppb)
Hall *et al.* (1976a)

appeared to be more evenly distributed throughout the basin since every sample contained PCB's and all but one contained DDT. The distribution of DDT and PCB's in four land use classifications of the basin is presented in Table 10. Residential and green space areas contained average concentrations of DDT between two and three times those found in industrial and commercial areas, implicating their use on lawns and gardens as one of the main sources of environmental contamination. In contrast, the highest concentrations of polychlorinated biphenyls were found in the commercial and industrial land use areas.

What are the relationships between the toxic substances in stream sediments and street surface contaminants? In most cases, the concentrations of trace metals found in street surface materials are higher than those found in stream sediments. Thus there is an apparent dilution of these materials caused by interdispersion with uncontaminated erosional sediments, leaching of trace metals into the water or deposition in other areas such as catch basins.

A comparison of locations of different contamination levels of street surface sediments to those in stream sediments can be made to determine if these materials remain close to their source of generation once they enter the aquatic environment or are distributed along the length of the stream. Some relationships are evident. For example, high concentrations of copper were found in the roadside materials from three industrial land use areas which are very close to the area of high copper concentrations found in the sediments of Still Creek. Values for most trace metals were lower on the greenspace areas of Burnaby Mountain coincident with very low values for stream sediments in these areas.

This comparison becomes much more difficult when non-point sources and atmospheric transport are involved in the generation and distribution of toxic materials. Notable examples are the internal combustion engine and the transportation network which appear to be a major source of lead in the environment. An attempt to collate the information on traffic flow and lead in street surface contaminants and stream sediments in order to assess the impact of the automobile upon lead distribution in the Brunette basin is presented in Figure 15. The vertical bars on this figure show the lead concentration in street surface contaminants from different land use areas and the circles indicate the range in

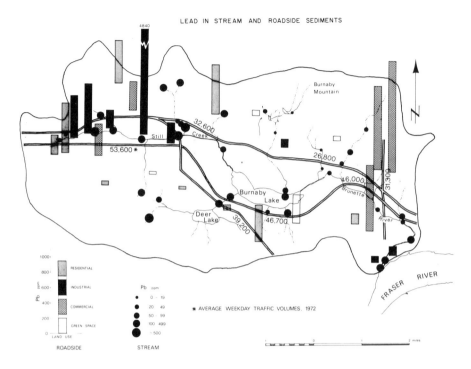

Figure 15   Source: Hall *et al.*, (1976a).

which the lead concentrations are found in stream sediments. The primary throughfares and their average weekday traffic volumes for 1972 are also presented on this map.

On Burnaby mountain, lead concentrations were low in both stream and roadside materials. Along Still Creek, where the two major traffic routes are close together, lead concentrations are very high in most samples from both streams and streets. However, at the east end of the lake where the highways are close together and the Pb concentrations are very high in street sediments from three commercial areas, the nearby sediments in the Brunette River show relatively low concentrations of lead. The lead concentrations do not appear to build up in the Brunette until the lower reaches, where incidentally very low concentrations are found in the adjacent street surface contaminants. These differences can be attributed to the hydraulic characteristics of the stream where the higher velocities in the upper reaches of the Brunette cause particulate lead generated in this area to be carried downstream and deposited in the slower flowing reaches of the river. Some of the residential areas near Deer Lake have very low concentrations of lead in street surface materials, but nearby streams have high concentrations. A possible explanation for this difference could be that the lead is not generated in this area, but is transported in the atmosphere from other high traffic density areas in Vancouver and is removed from the atmosphere into the streams during a rainfall event.

These are relatively simplistic interpretations which can be complicated by local traffic patterns, atmospheric circulation, seasonal climatic conditions and many other factors.

There was no obvious relationship between the location of high concentrations of chlorinated hydrocarbons in the stream and street sediments, suggesting that the flow characteristics in different reaches of the stream and the resultant sedimentation pattern controls the distribution of these toxic substances in the drainage basin.

SUMMARY AND CONCLUSIONS

The mountain tributaries are still in most cases of pristine quality for fish and recreational uses, while the small tributaries that drain the lowlands of the Fraser have poorer water quality than found in the mainstem Fraser. The impact of these lowland tributaries on the quality of water in the Fraser is very small, since they represent only a very minute proportion of the flow added to the Fraser below Hope and their load of pollutants is diluted very rapidly to Fraser River concentrations. However, one should keep in mind the biomagnification processes by which organisms may concentrate certain persistent pollutants that may be below our detection limits in the water.

Low dissolved oxygen concentrations which could affect fish populations have been measured in some reaches of the rural-agricultural basins. At several sites on the Salmon River, these depressed oxygen levels could be due to semi-point sources such as farmyard runoff.

High nutrient concentrations in the rural-agricultural basins provide the potential for excessive algal growth. On the Salmon River, higher nitrate concentrations are associated with low density residential developments, with septic tanks on coarse textured soil materials, rather than field cropping practices as had been anticipated.

The only toxic substances of significance in the rural-agricultural basin were the trace metals copper and zinc and the chlorinated hydrocarbon-polychlorinated biphenyl. The levels of copper and zinc were highest at high stream flow and sources appear to be related to occurrence of marine sediments and particularly residential developments and poultry production units. The polychlorinated biphenyls in the rural-agricultural tributaries appear to be associated with urbanized areas of the basin.

The Still Creek-Brunette River system contains high concentrations of toxic substances and large numbers of pathogens. Stormwater from urban areas is an important source of some trace metals, especially lead, and pathogens discharged to this urbanized waterway. Illegal connections of sanitary and industrial discharges to the storm sewers often increase the levels of contamination in stormwater.

Trace metals and chlorinated hydrocarbons are accumulating in sediments of this metropolitan basin. Their distribution in stream sediments is controlled by both land use activities and the hydraulic characteristics of the stream. Analysis of street sediments indicates that a variety of land use activities appear to be responsible for the generation of these toxic substances with the relative importance of each land use dependent upon the contaminant of concern.

The data collected on the Brunette system clearly demonstrate the importance of non-point sources as a cause of pollution in an urban-industrial region. There can be no doubt that if society is seriously interested in preserving the quality of the Lower Fraser, attention must be given to non-point sources of pollution and cannot be limited to pollutants that households and industries discharge to sewers or directly into the river.

REFERENCES

Benedict, A.H.; Hall, K.J.; and Koch, F.A., 1973. *A preliminary water quality survey of the Lower Fraser River system*. Technical Report no. 2. Westwater Research Centre, University of British Columbia, Vancouver.

Brown, G.W., 1974. *Forestry and water quality*. Oregon State University Bookstore, Corvallis, Oregon.

Ellis, B. and Childs, K.E., 1973. *Nutrient movement from septic tanks and lawn fertilization*. Technical Bulletin 73-5, Dept. of Natural Resources, Lansing, Michigan.

Geldreich, E.E. 1972. Water-borne pathogens. In *Water pollution microbiology,* ed. R. Mitchell, pp. 207-41. Wiley-Interscience, Toronto.

Greater Vancouver Sewerage and Drainage District. 1974. *Still Creek water quality report*. GVSDD, Vancouver.

Gustafson, C.G. 1970. PCB's — prevalent and persistent. *Environmental Science and Technology* 4:814-19.

Hall, K.J.; Koch, F.A.; and Yesaki, I. 1974. *Further investigations into water quality conditions in the Lower Fraser River*. Technical Report No. 4. Westwater Research Centre, University of British Columbia, Vancouver.

Hall, K.J.; Yesaki, I.; and Chan, J. 1976a. *Trace metals and chlorinated hydrocarbons in the sediments of a metropolitan watershed*. Westwater Research Centre, University of British Columbia, Vancouver. (In press).

Hall, K.J.; Isherwood, W.; and Fletcher, K. 1976b. *Distribution of trace metals in stream sediments of the Lower Fraser Valley*. Westwater Research Centre, University of British Columbia, Vancouver. (In preparation).

Hartman, G.F. 1968. *Growth rate and distribution of some fishes in the Chilliwack, South Alouette and Salmon Rivers*. Management Publication No. 11, B.C. Fish and Wildlife Branch, Victoria.

Hartman, G.F. and Gill, C.A., 1968. Distribution of juvenile steelhead and cutthroat trout [*Salmo gairdner and S. clarki clarki*] within streams in southwestern British Columbia. *J. Fish. Res. Bd. Canada* 25 (1): 33-48.

Inland Waters Branch. 1972. *Guidelines for water quality objectives and standards*. Technical Bulletin No. 67. Department of the Environment, Ottawa, Canada.

McMynn, R.G. and Vernon, E.H. 1954. *Physical and biological observations on the Salmon River - Fort Langley*. Management Report No. 13. B.C. Game Commission, Victoria.

Slaymaker, H.O. and Lavkulich, L.M. 1976. *Land use - water quality inter-relationships: a review and methodology.* Westwater Research Centre, University of British Columbia, Vancouver. (In preparation).

Wiens, J. and Beale, R. 1976. *Water quality in the Salmon River watershed: The relationship of land use and soil characteristics to water quality.* Westwater Research Centre, University of British Columbia, Vancouver. (In preparation).

Sawmill spans the mouth of the Brunette River.   Doug Miller

Gillnetting on the Fraser.   Finn Larsen

Snow Geese over Delta mudflats.   Brian Gates

5

Biology of the Lower Fraser and Ecological Effects of Pollution

by Thomas G. Northcote

Within sight, or nearly so, of the Lower Fraser River there are two inter-national fisheries agencies, a large federal fisheries management agency, three or more federal aquatic research laboratories, a provincial fisheries management agency, a provincial fisheries research laboratory, at least two major universities with strong backgrounds in freshwater and coastal marine biology, as well as several other institutions and organizations with interest in the ecology of this portion of the river. With such a powerhouse of biological expertise at the river's doorstep, some of it there for nearly half a century, one might assume that all of the basic biological work on the lower river was completed long ago and that we would now have a firm understanding of the more complex ecological inter-relationships between major components of this system, so essential for assessing and dealing with effects of pollution. To be sure, we do know a good deal about some fishes such as the salmon, and particularly with certain aspects of their migrant stages as they move down the river to oceanic feeding areas or back up the river to inland spawning grounds. But, paradoxical as it may seem, there are large sections of the biology of the Lower Fraser River about which, at least until very recently, we knew virtually nothing. And as annoying as it may be, especially to the taxpayers, still more information is probably required before it will be possible to predict with much certainty the ecological effects of pollution.

Herein I will briefly review the important biological stocks dependent on the Lower Fraser River, outline major features of its ecosystem (i.e. its key environmental components and some of its essential biological communities), summarize results of recent biological studies by Westwater on the river, and comment on how these may be used to indicate its present water quality condition. Finally, I will speculate on what all this implies for the biological future of the river.

BIOLOGICAL IMPORTANCE OF THE RIVER

Few people are unaware that the Fraser River is an important producer of Pacific salmon supporting not only major commercial, food and recreational fisheries but also providing a distinctive feature of British Columbian life. However probably not many appreciate the magnitude of the various stocks nor how critically dependent they all are upon the river at certain phases in their life history.

There are five different species of salmon in the eastern Pacific, and the Fraser has major runs of all five. Together they support a commercial fishery yielding an average annual catch valued at 45 million dollars (based on 1972 wholesale prices). Sockeye salmon have been the most important commercial species in the river, being fished by white man for well over 100 years and by native Indians for over 9000 years. Since the first commercial catch of a few thousand taken near Langley in 1829 the fishery rapidly expanded with the start of canneries in 1870 and by 1913 yielded over 30 million fish, probably the largest catch of salmon ever recorded anywhere. Following the disastrous rock dumping and slides of 1913 and 1914 at Hell's Gate in the Fraser canyon the catches declined drastically, but after completion of the Hell's Gate fishway and other management measures in the late 1940's runs on several of the cycle years have gradually improved. As a producer of sockeye salmon the Fraser now is second only to the Bristol Bay region in Alaska. On several years since the 1940's total runs of sockeye to the Fraser have exceeded 10 million fish and on most years they have been over a million.

Sizable runs of adult pink salmon enter the Fraser River only on alternate (odd numbered) years. Total runs of pink salmon bound for the river usually number over 2 million and on some years over 10 million fish. In recent years stocks of adult chum salmon from the Fraser have ranged from about a quarter million to over one-and-a-quarter million, averaging around one-half million fish annually whereas spawning stocks of chinook and coho salmon entering the river each probably have averaged slightly below a quarter million fish annually. Although runs of steelhead trout to the river are much smaller than those of salmon, the catch by sport fishermen has averaged over 10,000 fish from the system in recent years, suggesting a total stock of over 50,000 fish.

We all associate autumn with the up-river spawning migration of adult salmon, and spring with the downstream seaward migration of their young. However, when the timing of movement up and down the river is looked at more closely (Fig. 1) we see that the patterns are rather different for the various species. Considerable numbers of some species such as the chinook migrate upstream in the spring and summer while others such as the chum extend well into December. When the steelhead trout adults are also included it becomes obvious that there are many adult salmon and steelhead trout migrating up the river to spawn every day of the year. Indeed numbers usually exceed a thousand a day from mid June until late December and at times reach several hundred thousand daily (Fig. 2). Just when movement of adult salmon and steelhead up the river reaches its lowest level in early April, the downstream migration of young salmon and trout to the sea becomes maximal, with *several million* young moving down the river *each day* for most of April and May on some years. Except for January, February and part of December there are usually well over 10,000 salmon or steelhead migrating either up or down the river every day. Probably each time a person drives across the Port Mann bridge several of these fish are passing underneath, and at times there may be several hundred or thousand.

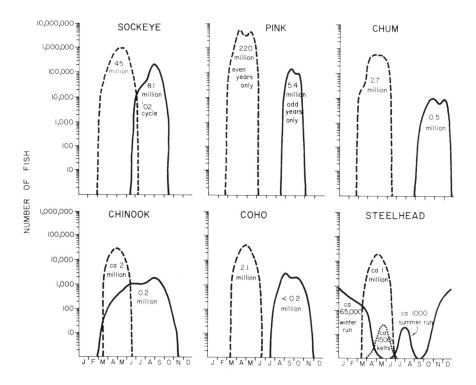

Figure 1 Generalized patterns of Pacific salmon and steelhead trout runs out of (young) and to (adults) the Fraser River.   Source: Northcote, (1974)

As abundant as the Fraser River salmon and steelhead still are, we know that stocks of several of the species have been considerably reduced since the early 1900's. This is certainly the case for some cycle years of sockeye salmon, for chum salmon, possibly for chinook and coho salmon as well as for steelhead trout. While catastrophic events such as the blockage at Hell's Gate may account for declines in stocks of some species, there are many other causes—some obvious and others not.

So far mention has been made only of the salmon and steelhead of the Fraser. In addition to these species there are several other migratory fishes such as sturgeon, eulachon, sea-run cutthroat trout and Dolly Varden, which have some commercial or sport fishing importance, as well as about 20 other species of fish which are either migratory, semi-migratory or resident in the river. These may have significant interactions with salmon and trout so should not be dismissed as unimportant.

Juvenile Salmon   Vancouver Public Aquarium

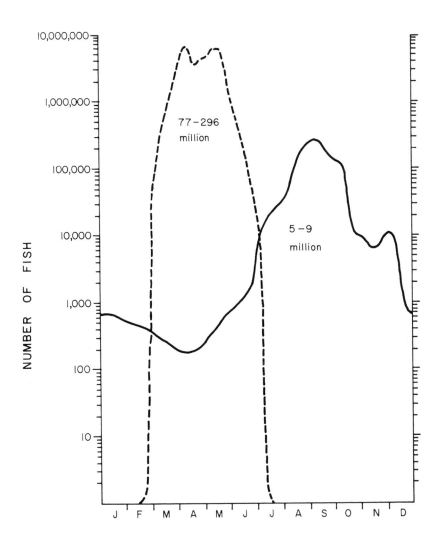

Figure 2 Generalized pattern of *average* runs of all Pacific salmon and steelhead trout from (young) and to (adults) the Fraser River. Range in total numbers depend on presence or absence of pink salmon young or adults as well as cyclic sockeye salmon adult runs (latter shown for an-02 cycle year).   Source: Northcote, (1974).

The Lower Fraser River and especially the marshes near its mouth also support an abundant and diverse fauna of aquatic birds. Nearly half of about 90 different species which live in close association with the river reside there more or less year round. In most regions of the Lower Fraser there are over 30 species of aquatic birds which utilize the river for breeding purposes and well over 40 species which winter there. Of the latter the swans, ducks and geese are of considerable importance. The river supports the largest wintering population of waterfowl in Canada, with numbers exceeding 100,000 in the estuary region alone.

In addition to fish and waterfowl there are many bottom dwelling invertebrates which inhabit the river banks, marshes and other areas of its shoreline or mouth. The small shrimp-like crustaceans and the aquatic insect larvae are important food sources for young salmon, trout and waterfowl. Furthermore there are large populations of clams, crabs and other shellfish living on the mudflats near the mouth of the river and these also are dependent to some extent on it for suitable habitat.

Even with this very incomplete and cursory survey of a few faunal groups utilizing the Lower Fraser, it has become obvious that the river supports populations of major importance not only to British Columbia but also to North America and indeed the world.

THE LOWER FRASER RIVER ECOSYSTEM

There are two features of paramount importance to the functioning of the Lower Fraser River ecosystem, both contained in its name. The first, of course, is that it *is* a river — a largely unidirectional *flowing* system. Major amounts of its dissolved nutrients and particulate organic materials must come largely from sources outside the main channel, especially from the surrounding land and vegetation. These nutrients and materials as well as many of the living organisms dependent upon them are continually entering and leaving the system at rates which not only vary enormously from year to year but also seasonally, daily, and even hourly, making studies and predictions most difficult.

The second most outstanding attribute of the system surely results from the location of the river section we have studied, namely its *lower* reaches. The lower reaches lie in the river floodplain with about 50 feet drop in elevation in the hundred miles between Hope and the river mouth so that deposition of fine particulates becomes much more significant than erosion, but not entirely so, as any farmer from the Lower Fraser Valley will testify! Nevertheless the assemblages of organisms inhabiting the river bottom and the fish spawning on it react to this change in substrate from the coarser erosional gravels in the up-river reaches to · the fine depositional sands and mud bottoms common in the lowermost sections.

Also of major impact on the ecosystem, and resulting from its "lower" location, is the river estuary. Here the unidirectional river flow takes on a complex two-directional pattern imposed by tides and wind action, with periodic intrusions of a salt water tongue some distance up the bottom of the river channels. Associated with this tongue is a quite distinctive flora and fauna of

Westham Island looking east.   Westwater

marine organisms, adding a further complexity to the river ecosystem. Furthermore, marshes and swamplands develop near the river mouth and these trap the
fine silts and organic materials carried down by the river, forming a highly
productive region with extensive beds of rooted aquatic plants, attached algae
and associated invertebrate animals — all extremely important for young migratory salmon and for waterfowl.

To complete this general overview of the Lower Fraser River ecosystem, a few
specific and some distinctive features should be noted. In the first place it is quite
a large river — rarely less than 20,000 cfs and at times approaching 500,000 cfs; a
fairly cold river — usually well below 15°C and almost never above 20°C; and a
very turbid river — transparency usually less than a metre and often less than half
a metre. These features strongly influence algal and aquatic plant production,
feeding and growth of aquatic animals and also the action of pollutant
additions. Secondly, the lower river is joined by a series of major tributaries as
well as a large number of smaller sloughs, backwaters and other important
waterways now extensively dyked, drained or otherwise cut off from the
mainstem river floodplain. Most of these used to serve and the few remaining still
do serve as important breeding or rearing areas for several species of fish and
waterfowl. Finally the river estuary does not open out into a large bay or a deep
protected inlet typical of many estuaries, but instead flows directly into the
marine waters of Georgia Strait, flanked on both sides by extensive shallow
mudflats and banks.

Canada Goose

Fitch Cady

Lower Fraser Valley farm

Westwater

WESTWATER'S FRASER RIVER BIOLOGICAL STUDIES

Detailed results of some of the biological studies by Westwater on the Lower Fraser River and banks at the river mouth are available in Technical Reports 1, 3, 7, 8, and 9 (see references); others will be forthcoming shortly. Only major aspects of this work will be summarized herein.

A series of 14 stations were established to sample the river biota in the Lower Fraser between its mouth and Hope, subjected as they are to quite contrasting land use development along this nearly 100 mile stretch (Fig. 3). Three stations (1, 2, 5) on the North Arm were located in a region of heavy urban and industrial development. Although similar development has occurred in some sections of the Main Arm, its extent is much less than in the North Arm and sizable areas adjacent to the river are utilized for agriculture. Three stations (3, 4, 6) were located along the Main Arm, two near its mouths and one about midway along it. Another three stations (7, 8, 9) were located between New Westminster and Whonock, representing a region of rapid change from a largely industrial and urban to a much more agricultural and forested mix of land use. Three more stations (10, 11, 12) between Mission City and Nicomen Island were located along an area of primarily agricultural land use with forested areas nearby. The remaining two stations (13, 14) were associated with large forested regions and small areas of agriculture.

At each of these stations the algal community attached (periphyton) to substrates on the river bottom, particularly log surfaces, was sampled as was that freely floating (phytoplankton) in the river water. Then the animals living in the mud, sand and other bottom materials along the river edge at depths up to about 10m were sampled with a bottom dredge. Those living near or at the mud-water interface were collected with a bottom sled towed for standard distances near shore (ca 1.5m deep), offshore (ca 4-5m deep) and near mid-river (usually 6-8m deep). Animals drifting downstream near the river surface were sampled near shore and mid-river with both fine (0.35mm) and coarse mesh (1.18mm) tow nets. The near-shore fish community was sampled on each occasion by at least two standard seine hauls and gill net sets at each station (10 mesh sizes from 25-140mm stretched mesh). Sampling was conducted at four different times at each station (late summer - early autumn, 1972; late autumn - winter 1972; spring 1973; summer 1973).

In addition to the above sampling programme on the river proper, a quantitative survey was made of the benthic organisms living in the mudflats of Sturgeon and Roberts banks at the mouth of the river during the summer of 1972 (Bawden et al., 1973).

The Algal Community

Obvious concentration zones of attached algae were evident a short distance beneath the surface at most stations in the lower mainstem river (Stations 7-9) and particularly in the river arms. At times algal biomass approached 20mg/cm^2 (ash-free dry weight) in the river arms but was much lower at the middle and upper mainstem stations, rarely exceeding 6mg/cm^2.

Diatoms were the dominant attached algal group, being represented by some 112 different species of which only about 20 were common. Attached diatoms reached maximum abundance along the river at the North Arm river mouth stations in spring (up to about 12 million cells/cm^2) but otherwise numbers usually ranged between 0.5 and 4.5 million cells/cm^2 at most other stations. Twenty-two species of green algae were recorded from the river periphyton, along with six species of blue-green algae, none of which were common. The attached algal community of the Lower Fraser River, especially that in the lowermost reaches was quite abundant compared to that of several other river and lake systems, including some which were moderately productive or even polluted. However sampling techniques were not comparable in all of these studies, making comparisons difficult.

The phytoplanktonic community of the Lower Fraser River was very sparse at all stations as might be expected in this fairly swiftly flowing, cold and turbid river. Even during the spring bloom period cell numbers infrequently exceeded 200/ml, well below that reported for the lower Columbia River.

The Bottom Fauna Community

The benthic organisms living within the river bottom appeared to be at least 10 times more abundant than the epibenthic forms associated with the mud-water interface (Fig. 4). Nevertheless both these communities showed a similar change in numbers and biomass along the length of the Lower Fraser with maximum values in the North Arm and minimums in the mainstem river, especially in upper reaches. In the Main Arm and along much of the river upstream from New Westminster the numbers and biomass of the benthic community seemed fairly similar to that reported in other large temperate rivers of North America and Europe.

Although relatively few of the organisms were identified as to species, most were taken to genus, giving a total of 82 taxa for the benthic community and 104 in the epibenthic community. There were essentially 5 different patterns of abundance shown by major groups of the benthic fauna (Fig. 5), as well as the epibenthic fauna, along the Lower Fraser River. Several marine or estuarine forms, illustrated by the amphipod "shrimps" (and also by polychaete and nemertine worms, leeches and molluscs — not shown) were most abundant in the river arms but were very limited or absent entirely from the mainstem river. Mysid "shrimps" were present from the river mouth almost to the uppermost station but in much reduced numbers towards the upper reaches. Two major groups, the oligochaete worms and the dipteran midge fly larvae were moderately abundant along the whole length of the Lower Fraser, the former most abundant in the lowermost reaches and the latter in the uppermost reaches. In a fifth pattern of distribution, illustrated by mayfly, caddisfly and stonefly nymphs, the organisms were absent from most estuarine stations and reached maximum abundance further up the mainstem river.

The macrofauna associated with the Sturgeon and Roberts bank mudflats contained over 50 different species, including 7 bivalves, 2 snails, 9 crabs and

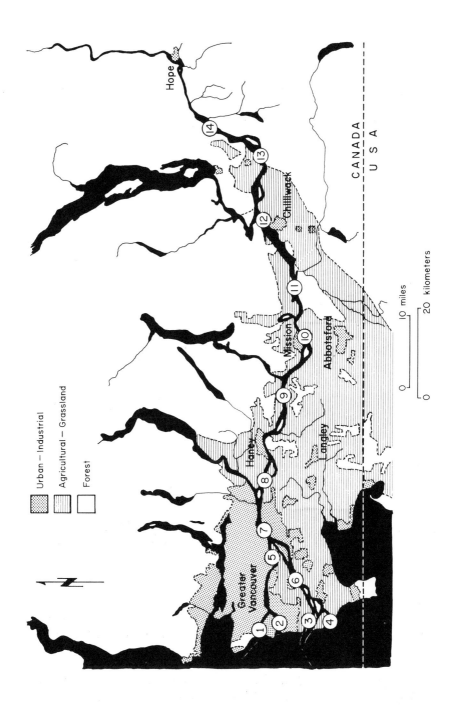

Figure 3   Location of 14 biological sampling stations.

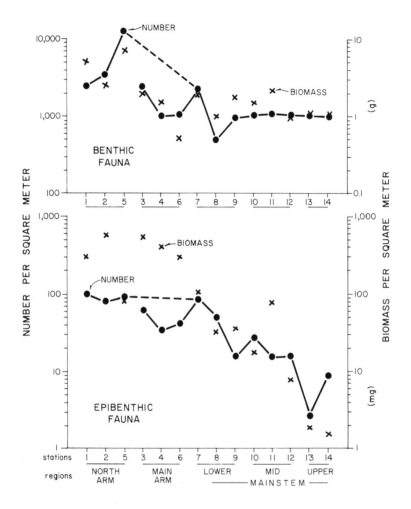

Figure 4 Regional changes in the average abundance and biomass of the benthic and epibenthic fauna of the Lower Fraser River. Broken line between station 5 & 7 indicates their close geographical location.   Source: Northcote *et al.*, (1976a)

shrimp, 3 amphipods, an isopod and 20 polychaete worms. The meiofauna consisted mainly of oligochaete and nematode worms along with considerable numbers of harpacticoid copepods, particularly in the near surface layer.

The Drift Fauna

Although at least 81 different taxa were recorded in the samples of organisms drifting down near the surface of the river, the macroinvertebrate forms were surprisingly sparse (about one per 100m^3) with little change in abundance

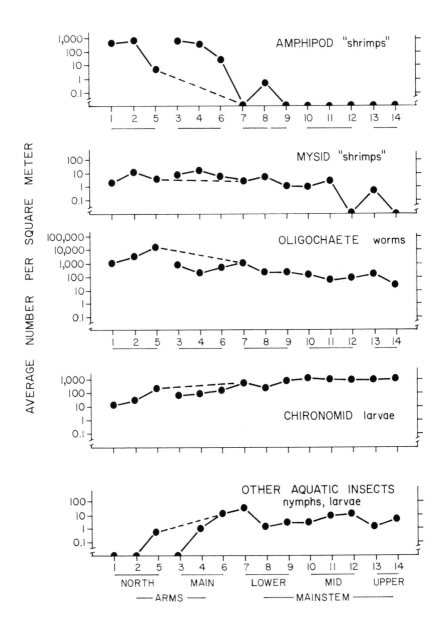

Figure 5 Regional changes in average abundance of major groups of benthic invertebrates of the Lower Fraser River.   Source: Northcote *et al.*, (1976a)

regionally. Smaller invertebrates, largely zooplankton and insect larvae were somewhat more abundant, especially near the river mouth where numbers occasionally exceeded one organism per m^3.

The Fish Community

Some 34 different species of fish were found in the Lower Fraser River during our study. Considering that there are only about 70 species of freshwater fish in all of British Columbia, the fauna of the river is reasonably diverse, although a few of the 34 are marine species which were only found at stations near the river mouth. These include Pacific herring, surf smelt, staghorn and manacled sculpins as well as the shiner perch. The starry flounder, also a marine fish but one quite tolerant of freshwater, was one of the most common fishes in seine hauls as far upstream as Whonock and on occasions was taken at Mission City (Station 10).

As might be expected the migratory fishes were taken at most of the stations along the river. About a dozen species would be included in this group – namely the white sturgeon, eulachon, longfin smelt, all five species of Pacific salmon, rainbow and cutthroat trout, Dolly Varden and the threespine stickleback. Of the "resident" forms, three species stand out as dominant in the Lower Fraser, at least as indicated by our sampling techniques. These are the largescale sucker, the peamouth chub and the prickly sculpin. Each of these species was taken in abundance at all stations almost every time we sampled. Also occurring at all stations along the river was the northern squawfish, but not so frequently or as abundantly as the other three species.

Several of the fish species of the Lower Fraser seem to be up-river forms, or at least are much more abundant in those regions. Included here are redside shiners, leopard dace and mountain whitefish. Although the latter occur right down to the river mouth in both the North and Main arms they do not seem to be as common there as at the middle and upper mainstem stations.

A few species such as the carp, the brassy minnow, the burbot or freshwater codfish, the black crappie and the Aleutian sculpin were taken too infrequently to say much about their distribution along the river. Surprisingly the brown bullhead or catfish which I know to be common in several areas of the Lower Fraser was only taken once in our study.

Although sampling variability was large, some major trends were evident in the relative abundance of fish in different regions of the river (Fig. 6, 7). In both the gillnet and seine catches the total abundance and biomass of fish tended to be slightly larger in the upper reaches of the mainstem river than in the lower mainstem or the river arms. However, differences between regions in the total catches were usually less than an order of magnitude. Marine species, especially for the seined fish, made up a substantial fraction of the total catch in the river arms, but these declined rapidly in the mainstem river. The contribution of salmonoid fishes (salmon, trout, char and whitefish) to the fish catch was rather low in the river arms, and especially so in the North Arm. The average salmonoid catch at Station 5 (middle of North Arm) in both numbers and

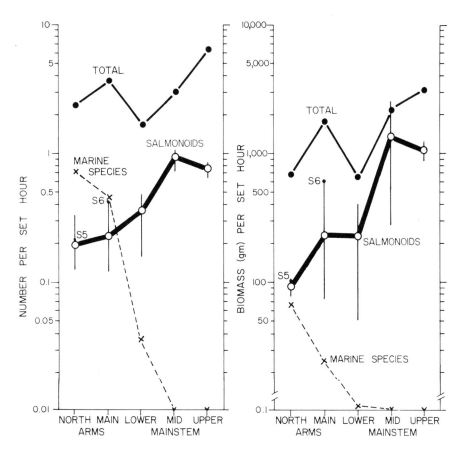

Figure 6 Regional changes in the average gillnet catch of fish from the Lower Fraser River. Data averaged for all stations within each region. (S5 indicates station 5 on the North Arm and S6, station 6 on the Main Arm)   Source: Northcote *et al.*, (1976b)

biomass was consistently much less than that at Station 6 (middle of Main Arm) for both the gillnet (Fig. 6) and seine data (Fig. 7). Salmonoid catches were highest in the mid-upper mainstem reaches of the river.

The utilization by fish of marsh habitat near the mouth of the North and Main arms of the river was studied at bi-weekly intervals during the spring and summer of 1973 and 1974, largely by seining. Two types of habitat were recognized, sloughs and side-channels. Eleven stations representing slough habitat were established, five in the North Arm near Swishwash Island and six in the Duck-Barber-Ladner marsh area of the Main Arm. Four different stations in the latter area were selected to represent side-channel habitat. At least 18 species

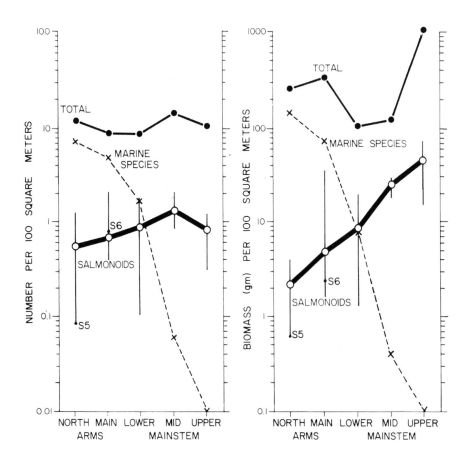

Figure 7 Regional changes in the average seine catch of fish from the Lower Fraser River. Data averaged for all stations within each region.

Source: Northcote *et al.*, (1976b)

of fish inhabited the marsh waters including two marine forms, the staghorn sculpin and the starry flounder, both of which were common there. Other common forms were peamouth chub, threespine stickleback, prickly sculpin and young of two species of salmon—chum and chinook. The latter were taken in large numbers (Fig. 8) throughout much of the spring and summer period in 1973 as well as in 1974. The abundance of these species of young salmon in the marsh areas was several times greater than that recorded by similar sampling techniques in the river arms, emphasizing the importance of marsh regions as temporary rearing habits for these salmonids. Timing of occurrence and growth characteristics of these young salmon suggest that they may utilize the

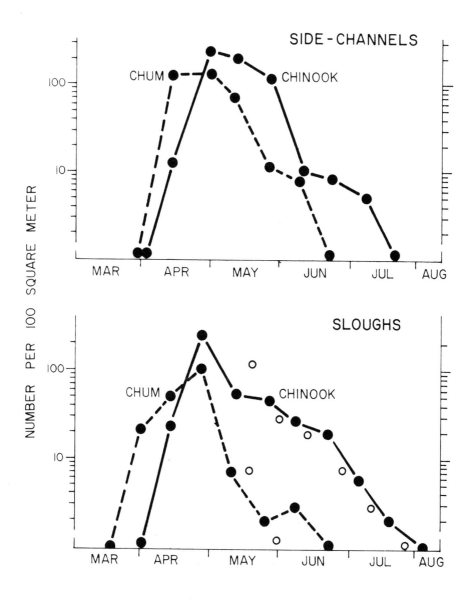

Figure 8 Seasonal changes (1973) in abundance of young chum and chinook salmon utilizing marsh habitat of the Lower Fraser River. Large solid dots for Main Arm, small open dots for North Arm sampling stations.

Source: Dunford, (1975)

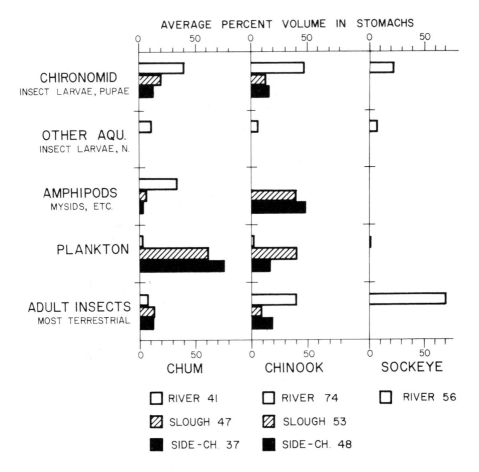

Figure 9 Major food sources of young chum, chinook and sockeye salmon from different feeding habitats of the Lower Fraser River. Numbers after habitat types give fish sample size; data in part from Dunford, 1975.

Source: Northcote *et al.*, (1976c)

marshes for at least a few weeks (chum) and possibly up to several months (chinook). Similar densities of young chum and chinook salmon were found in the slough habitats at the mouth of the North Arm and in the Main Arm during the period when both areas were sampled (Fig. 8).

The food web of the fish community of the Lower Fraser River will be summarized very briefly by examining diets of two major groups — the young migratory salmon, and the less migratory ("resident") forms. Two species of young salmon, chum and chinook, feed extensively in sloughs and side-channel areas in addition to the mainstem river and its arms (Fig. 9). In the main river channel the young chum salmon depend heavily on benthic prey (especially chironomid insect larvae) and on small crustaceans. In the slough and side-channel habitats zooplankton becomes a more important food source along with adult insects. Both of these items are much more abundant in the slow moving, productive marsh areas than in the mainstem river or its arms. Young chinook salmon which feed largely on chironomid insect larvae in the main river turn much more to amphipods, mysids and other benthic crustaceans in the sloughs and side-channels. Young sockeye in the river feed mainly on young and adult stages of insects as well as zooplankton. Neither they nor the young pink nor coho salmon utilize the marsh areas for feeding to any extent.

The five species representing the less migratory or "resident" fishes of the Lower Fraser all relied to a considerable extent on insects produced on the river bottom (Fig. 10). Most of these fishes showed obvious changes in diet between young of the year (fry) and older stages, plankton usually being much more important in the fry and fish being so in adults of some species, notably the

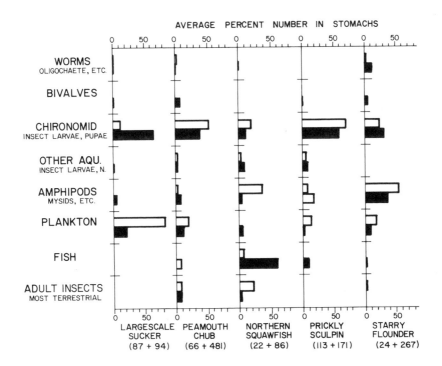

Figure 10 Major food sources of young (open bars) and subadult-adult (solid bars) resident fishes common in the Lower Fraser River. Numbers in parenthesis give sample size of young and subadult-adult fish, respectively.

Source: Northcote *et al.*, (1976c)

squawfish. Mysids were commonly taken by young flounder and squawfish whereas aquatic worms and bivalves were rarely utilized, except perhaps by flounder and chub.

BIOLOGICAL WATER QUALITY INDICATORS

The complexities of the Fraser River ecosystem, combined with the introduction of major sources of pollution just in those regions of the river where estuarine influences are also being expressed, makes attempts to recognize biological indicators of water pollution extremely difficult. But however concerned we are with water quality *per se* in the river, surely the biological effects are of paramount interest and importance to us. In the following pages an attempt, albeit cautiously, will be made to look for biological early warning signs of environmental degradation in the river communities.

Indicator Species or Groups

In the beginning phases of the ecological vogue there was much ado as well as abuse of the indicator species concept. Yet to many it still seems reasonable that, if carefully and cautiously interpreted, the occurrence of certain forms in a habitat can provide considerable insight into conditions prevailing there. Characteristics of the attached algae and the benthic invertebrates make them more useful than other communities as water quality indicators but the fish community will also be examined briefly in this regard.

Of the many species of attached diatom algae in the Lower Fraser there are forms such as *Achnanthes minutissima,* commonly considered to be representative of relatively unpolluted water, which are common and widely distributed along the system. But there also are other forms frequently associated with much more eutrophic (i.e. enriched) conditions, such as *Diatoma vulgare* and *Gomphonema parvulum,* which also are common and widespread. The attached green alga *Cladophora glomerata* is a species well known elsewhere in British Columbia, in Canada and in England for indicating highly eutrophic or polluted conditions. In the Lower Fraser we found it at all stations in the river arms and at several along the mainstem river, but most consistently and abundantly at Station 5 in the middle of the North Arm and at Station 7 near New Westminster. Happenstance perhaps, and yet . . .? Of the several algal species which commonly occurred in the middle or upper mainstem sections of the river none was recorded as being a pollution indicator.

Two broad categories of reaction to pollution were recognized for the benthic macroinvertebrates of the Lower Fraser, namely "tolerant" and "sensitive" forms. Three groups were designated tolerant to organic pollution—the oligochaete worms, the leeches and the psychodids (larvae of the dipteran sand and moth flies). Sensitive forms included mayfly and stonefly nymphs, caddisfly larvae and larvae of 13 different genera of chironomids (midge flies). Marked differences in the relative abundance of these forms were evident at the various stations along the river (Fig. 11). Of the pollution tolerant forms, the oligochaetes were clearly far more abundant in the river arms, and especially at Station 5 in the middle of

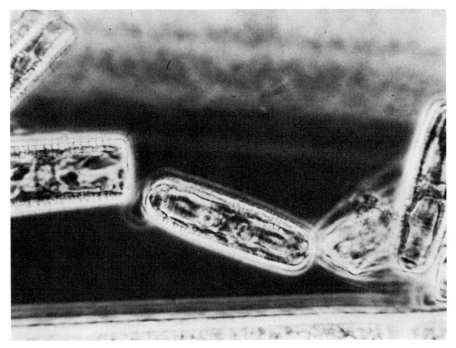

Diatoma vulgare   Gordon Ennis

the North Arm, than at most mainstem river stations except 7 (New West-minster). The leeches and psychodids also appeared to be restricted to river arm stations, the leeches being most abundant at Station 5 in the North Arm. Of the sensitive forms, chironomids were least abundant in the river arm stations and much more abundant in the middle-to-upper mainstem stations. Aversion for saline conditions may well explain the low numbers of chironomids at the river mouth (Stations 1 - 4) but probably not why the average number at Station 5 was about three times less than at Station 6. Maximum salinities at Station 6 were about 20 times higher than those at Station 5, so if salinity avoidance were a major factor it should have restricted chironomid abundance much more at Station 6 than at Station 5, quite the opposite of what was actually observed. Stoneflies, caddisflies and mayflies were not recorded in samples from the river arms and reached maximum average densities in the middle or upper mainstem reaches (Fig. 11).

Turning to the fishes of the Lower Fraser, these show no simple or obvious patterns of distribution, growth or other characteristics which clearly designate regions of pollution. All of the salmonoid species (mountain whitefish, chinook, chum and sockeye salmon, rainbow and cutthroat trout as well as Dolly Varden) which were commonly found at Station 6 in the middle of the Main Arm were also taken at Station 5 in the middle of the North Arm, although usually in somewhat lower numbers as noted previously (Fig. 6,7).

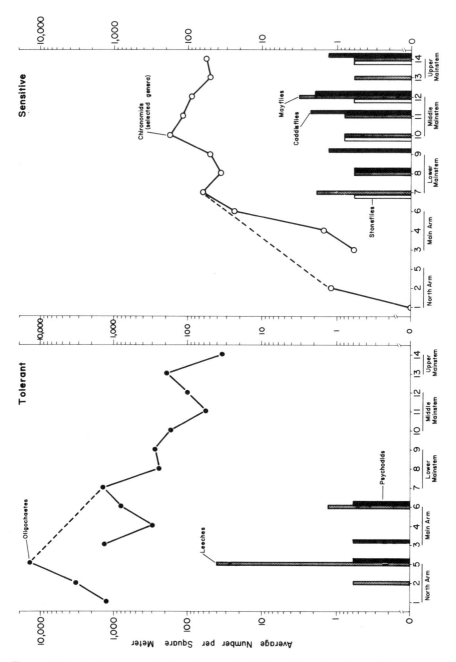

Figure 11 Regional changes in abundance of pollution tolerant and sensitive forms of benthic macroinvertebrates in the Lower Fraser River.

Source: Northcote *et al.*, (1976)

Species Diversity

A common response of biological communities to effects of pollution is for the total number of different species to decrease and for a few pollution tolerant species to become particularly abundant. On the surface then, it would seem that an index which would in some way respond both to a reduction in number of species and the tendency for a few of these to become much more abundant would be a most useful pollution indicator. Several such diversity indices have been developed and used. However, factors other than stress on a community by pollution may cause a low species diversity index. For example, a very unproductive aquatic community may have a low species diversity but in no way be polluted. Also other stresses, such as those imposed by increased salinity, may reduce diversity. Obviously once again care must be used in interpretation, but this holds for most characteristics of biological systems. A commonly used diversity index is the Shannon-Wiener function which ranges from values well below 1 for a very low diversity community as occurs in polluted waters, to values well over 2 in many unpolluted rivers. A further extension of the Shannon-Wiener diversity function permits calculation of an "equitability" index, i.e. the degree to which the total number of individuals in a community are evenly distributed between the various species (or taxa). Equitability indices are generally above 0.5 for benthic invertebrate communities of unpolluted streams in southeastern U.S.A.

Obviously for any community to reflect to best advantage through its species diversity the effects of pollutant stress, it should be relatively immobile (i.e. not easily able to respond by avoiding periodic or intermittent stresses). Furthermore it preferably should not respond markedly or quickly to minor changes in pollution but yet serve as a sensitive summator of ambient environmental conditions. Thus diversity indices calculated from fish communities usually would not be expected to reflect anything but very severe and gross pollution whereas those determined from attached algal communities might be more useful and those from benthic invertebrates perhaps most sensitive.

Separate Shannon-Wiener species diversity functions were calculated for the fish community at each of the five regions of the Lower Fraser (North Arm, Main Arm, lower, middle and upper mainstem) for both the gillnet and seine data. All showed species diversity values well above 2, the lowest (2.339) being for seine-caught fish at the North Arm stations. Similarily the values determined for the attached diatom communities at the various stations were usually greater than 2 with only occasionally lower values at a few river arm stations, never consistently any particular one.

Diversity indices for benthic invertebrate communities of nearly all lower Fraser River stations were well above 1 and equitability indices well above 0.5 (Fig. 12), except for one notable exception — at Station 5 in the middle of the North Arm. Here no doubt the great preponderance of oligochaete worms in the benthic fauna markedly reduced both diversity and equitability.

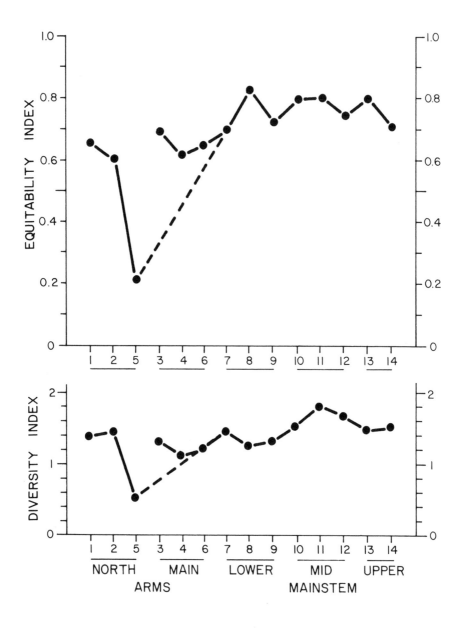

Figure 12 Regional changes in the average diversity (Shannon-Wiener function) and equitability of the benthic fauna of the Lower Fraser River.

Source: Northcote *et al.*, (1976a)

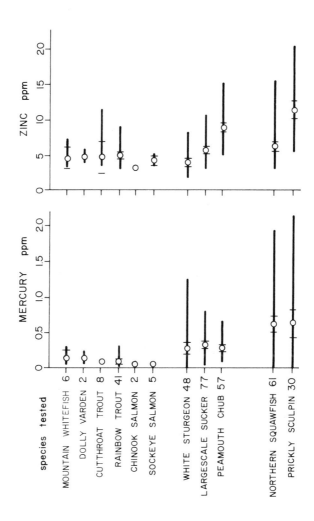

Figure 13 Concentrations of mercury and zinc (wet weight white muscle tissue) in fishes from the Lower Fraser River. Horizontal lines indicate ranges, circles - averages, short vertical bars - 5 percent fiducial limits. Numbers in front of species give sample size.   Source: Northcote *et al.*, (1975a)

Biological Uptake of Contaminants

Nowadays concern over biological uptake and concentration of contaminant materials such as heavy metals and pesticides has become widespread and even frequent household topics of conversation. In many ways this facilitates appreciation of the use such biomagnification may have in assessing pollutant stress, long before the loads accumulated may have very serious consequences to their carriers or to humans consuming them. This in no way ignores the dangers which sublethal concentrations may impart to aquatic organisms.

Concentrations of 11 trace elements (most of them heavy metals) were analyzed in some 350 specimens of subadult or adult fish, representing 14 different species from the 14 stations along the Lower Fraser River. Except for mercury, no significantly high concentration of any of these trace elements was found in the muscle tissue of the various species. However some species tended to have very low and others much higher levels as is illustrated by mercury and zinc (Fig. 13). The salmonoid fishes (whitefish, Dolly Varden, trout and salmon) all had very low values, probably a result of the fact that several of these species spend little time in the river and others are not top carnivores there. The Dolly Varden and cutthroat trout might have been expected to have had higher trace metal loads as both are heavy fish eaters, but the individuals tested may have been sea-run forms. Three species — white sturgeon, largescale sucker and peamouth chub — are commonly but not exclusively river resident species which at times feed heavily on benthic food sources. Most of these have slightly higher concentrations of mercury and zinc (Fig. 13). Northern squawfish and prickly sculpin, the two species which stay entirely within the river and which feed largely at or near the top of the food web, have even higher trace metal concentrations.

There was no evidence that fish from any particular region of the Lower Fraser River had especially high concentrations of any of the trace elements, as was clearly shown by the data for mercury (Fig. 14). This does not necessarily mean that there are not localized sources of contamination in the lower river, because the fish may well move about between regions to a considerable extent — some, such as the sturgeon, no doubt moving much more than others.

The occurrence of mercury concentrations well above the accepted level in Canadian food (0.5ppm) in several of the species, especially the northern squawfish, where *average* concentrations in all regions were over 0.5ppm, certainly demands explanation. This cannot be provided until further studies on mercury levels in Fraser River sediments are completed, various possible sources of contamination are checked and the general background concentrations in the system established.

Perhaps a clearer pattern of trace metal contamination is shown by the shellfish at the mouth of the Fraser River. Highest levels were found in specimens taken from mudflats at the mouth of the North Arm, as is well illustrated by mercury concentrations in commercial crabs (Fig. 15). A major source of heavy metals here may be discharge from the Vancouver sewage treatment plant which empties out onto Sturgeon Bank off the mouth of the North Arm.

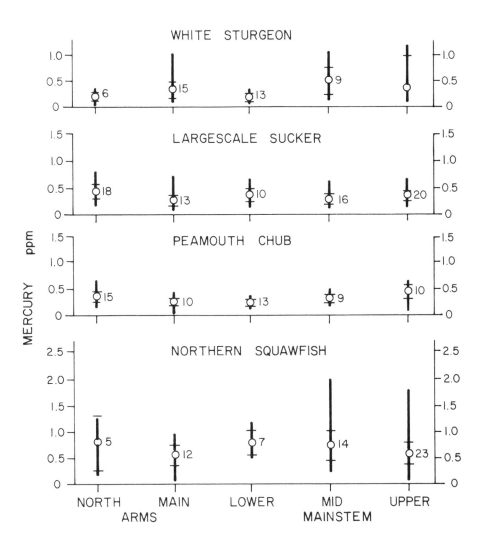

Figure 14 Regional changes in concentrations of mercury in white muscle tissue of fishes from the Lower Fraser River. Symbols as in Fig. 13; numbers beside average give sample size.   Source: Northcote *et al.*, (1975a)

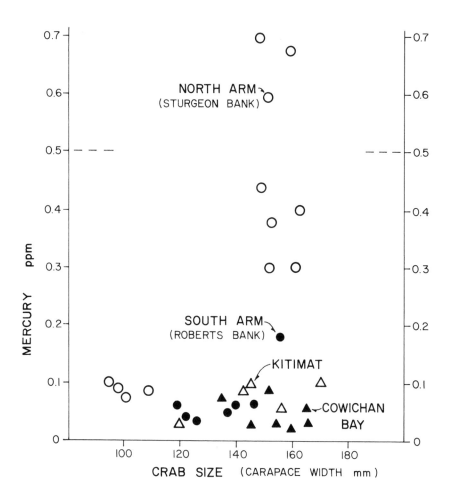

Figure 15 Regional and size changes in concentrations of mercury (wetweight, muscle tissue) in commercial crabs from the mouth of the North and Main Arms of the Lower Fraser River. Samples from two other regions of coastal British Columbia given for comparison.

Source: Bawden *et al.*, (1973) and Parsons *et al.*, (1973)

Of the 11 different forms of chlorinated hydrocarbons tested for in nearly 200 specimens of fish from the Lower Fraser, three were found in nearly 80 per cent of the individuals. These were heptachlor epoxide, PCB's (polychlorinated biphenyls) and DDT and its breakdown products. Northern squawfish again usually had the highest loads, and in this species the maximum concentrations of all three forms were invariably found in those specimens taken from the river arms (Fig. 16).

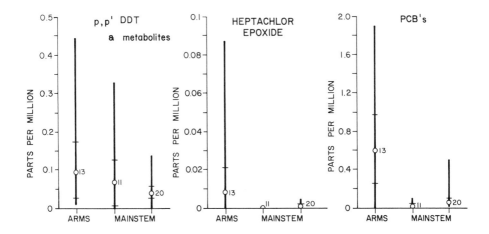

Figure 16 Concentrations of major chlorinated hydrocarbon contaminants found in white muscle tissue of northern squawfish from designated regions of the lower Fraser River. Symbols as in Fig. 14.
Source: Albright *et al.*, (1975) and Johnston *et al.*, (1975)

SUMMARY AND CONCLUSIONS

Several ecological effects of pollution on the Lower Fraser River have been noted and others surely implied. These now need to be drawn together, assessed and where possible related to future changes. Only the important or obvious effects, and especially those which have significant impacts on salmon, wildlife and man will be considered here.

One of the first and most obvious points to be made is that there are marked differences evident in the signs of pollution along the length of the Lower Fraser. However it is easier to see or smell signs of pollution than it is to assess their effects. Furthermore, those signs of pollution which attack our sensitivities most vigorously may sometimes be relatively innocuous compared to others which pass by unnoticed. Who for example can see, smell, or taste mercury, PCB's or pesticides at part per billion concentrations in fish?

High mercury levels were found in Sturgeon Bank crabs.

Peter Kellington and Larry Berg

But how positive is our evidence for regional localization of pollution along the Lower Fraser? At various levels in the biological community of the river we have seen evidence that the river arms and particularly certain areas of the North Arm are showing changes which may be the result of pollution. This was shown in the abundance and species composition of the attached algae as well as that of the benthic and epibenthic invertebrate community. It was also evident in the various diversity indices which were determined, notably again those for the bottom dwelling organisms. As for the heavy metal contaminants (at least those in benthic communities at the river mouth) and the chlorinated hydrocarbon residues in fish, there were obviously higher loads being taken up by the fauna living in the lower reaches of the river compared to those further upstream. While some of these changes may be related to estuarine or marine influence near the river mouth, this is an insufficient explanation as a comparison of maximum salinity data between the North and Main Arm stations clearly shows. Furthermore, the relative pollution loading to the North Arm at Station 5 is well over 10 times that to the Main Arm at Station 6 (1973 data) even if the load from above New Westminster is neglected, which if anything would further increase that to the North Arm. With some (but severe) limitations we might even use features of the North Arm to indicate possible future effects on other regions of the lower river; not a charming prospect!

To many, one of the major threats to life in the Fraser River would seem to be that from the various chemicals entering with industrial or domestic wastewater inflows. We have seen that in the river, like in many other aspects of life, there is no "safe period"—no time of the year when a lethal spill might avoid killing thousands or more of salmonids if it was widespread across the river flow or even localized in certain critical areas. As terrifying as such a catastrophe would appear to be, the slow but steady attrition of the salmonid populations which may result from even temporary exposure to sublethal concentrations of pollutants seems to me a far greater danger. Who notices if young salmon, slightly stunned by briefly passing through a small inflow of toxicant discharge on their downstream migration, cannot avoid so effectively the many predators awaiting them at the river mouth? Who cares if adult salmon, fighting up the inland river rapids can't quite reach their home spawning grounds — surely they can spawn somewhere else, and don't they all die after spawning anyway? But in terms of maintaining the populations, the result is the same as if all these fish had been killed outright by a lethal dose of pollutant.

The levels at which some of these contaminants can seriously impair normal body functions or behaviour is surprisingly low. For example, egg concentrations of DDT or PCB's in the range of a hundred or so *parts per billion* in adult salmonids, which in no way kills them, may nevertheless considerably reduce survival of their young. Other more subtle effects on swimming speed and balance or impairment of sensory perception occur at a range of toxicant concentrations from parts per billion to a few parts per million.

Unfortunately some pollution "clean-up" practices may produce materials more toxic to organisms than the primary pollutants themselves. A disturbing example of this is found in the chloramine compounds formed by chlorination at sewage treatment plants. The chlorinate residuals may persist in sewage effluents, at lethal levels to young salmonids for more than two days. Furthermore chlorination from treatment plants has been shown to depress the photosynthetic activity and respiration of planktonic algal populations, which could have serious effects on productivity of marshes or of marine ecosystems off the river mouth.

There are also many uncertainties and dangers present in special regions of the river, particularly the marsh, slough and backwater habitats along its margins and near its mouth. As we have seen, some species of young salmon do not move as quickly out of the river in their seaward migration as was once thought, but instead reside temporarily in sloughs and marsh areas during vulnerable phases of adjustment to higher salinites. The Duck-Woodward-Barber Island complex near the mouth of the Main Arm of the river serves as a rearing and feeding zone for large numbers of chum and chinook salmon juveniles. In such regions the flushing rate of pollutants may be much slower than in the mainstem river or its arms so that exposure times are increased, intensifying harmful effects. Also these habitats usually present a very untidy, disorganized appearance, apparently clamouring for tidying up, straightening out or other forms of modern "development". Yet beneath their seeming disarray is a highly productive and vitally important ecosystem not only to the young salmonids but also to the populations of waterfowl which use the region intensively. In addition, the marshes and associated wetlands are receiving much interest recently in their role as valuable natural treatment systems for various nutrients, wastes and contaminants associated with adjacent development by man.

Finally, in our preoccupation with the Lower Fraser, we must not forget that this is only one small part of a much larger system. Water quality conditions in a few of its tributaries are discussed elsewhere in this volume. But there are many larger tributaries both in the Lower Fraser drainage basin itself, as well as further upstream. These cannot be ignored because their condition sets the stage for much of the "biology" we find in lower reaches of the river. Effects of upriver environmental degradation may all too quickly be swept downstream to be expressed even more broadly.

Thus we have seen that the biological future of the Lower Fraser is fraught with many uncertainties, many of which fortunately we seem to have in our control, but not necessarily *in control*. With all of these uncertainties there is at least this one certainty. On the Lower Fraser River we still have time and the technical capability of maintaining those large and important populations of fish and waterfowl at more or less their present levels if not at ones considerably greater. How much longer we can still have this certainty however is by no means clear.

REFERENCES

Albright, L.J.; Northcote, T.G.; Oloffs, P.C.; and Szeto, S.Y. 1975. Chlorinated hydrocarbon residues in fish, crabs, and shellfish of the Lower Fraser River, its estuary, and selected locations in Georgia Strait. *Pesticides Monitoring Journal.* 9:134-140.

Bawden, C.A.; Heath, W.A.; and Norton, A.B. 1973. *A preliminary baseline study of Roberts and Sturgeon Banks.* Technical Report no. 1. Westwater Research Centre, University of British Columbia, Vancouver.

Dunford, W.E. 1975. *Space and food utilization by salmonids in marsh habitats of the Fraser River Estuary.* M.Sc. Thesis. Dept. of Zoology, University of British Columbia, Vancouver.

Johnston, N.T.; Albright, L.J.; Northcote, T.G.; Oloffs, P.C.; and Tsumura, K. 1975. *Chlorinated hydrocarbon residues in fishes from the Lower Fraser River.* Technical Report no. 9. Westwater Research Centre, University of British Columbia, Vancouver.

Northcote, T.G. 1974. *Biology of the Lower Fraser River: A Review.* Technical Report no. 3. Westwater Research Centre, University of British Columbia, Vancouver.

Northcote, T.G.; Johnston, N.T.; and Tsumura, K. 1975(a) *Trace metal concentrations in Lower Fraser River fishes.* Technical Report no. 7. Westwater Research Centre, University of British Columbia, Vancouver.

Northcote, T.G.; Ennis, G.L., and Anderson, M.H. 1975(b) *Periphytic and planktonic algae of the Lower Fraser River in relation to water quality conditions.* Technical Report no. 8. Westwater Research Centre, University of British Columbia, Vancouver.

Northcote, T.G.; Johnston, N.T.; and Tsumura, K. 1976(a). *Benthic, Epi-benthic, and Drift Fauna of the Lower Fraser River.* (In preparation).

Northcote, T.G.; Johnston, N.T.; and Tsumura, K. 1976(b). *Distribution, Abundance, Size, and Growth of Fishes from the Lower Fraser River.* (in preparation).

Northcote, T.G.; Johnston, N.T.; and Tsumura, K. 1976(c). *Feeding Studies on Fishes from the Lower Fraser River.* (in preparation).

Parsons, T.R.; Bawden, C.A.; and Heath, W.A. 1973. Preliminary survey of mercury and other metals contained in animals from the Fraser River. *J. Fish. Res. Bd. Canada* 30:1014 — 1016.

Fitch Cady

Doug Miller

6

Implementing Pollution Control

by Anthony H.J. Dorcey

In the preceding chapters we have described water quality conditions in the Lower Fraser, the pollutants that should be cause for concern, their many sources and the diverse pathways by which they reach the tributaries and main stream. The conclusions reached in the chapters so far may be summarized as follows:

First of all, what are the pollutants we should be concerned about? Whilst the mainstream of the Lower Fraser is in relatively good condition compared with many other heavily-used rivers in the world, it is presently degraded by high numbers of pathogens and there are indications that significant accumulations of toxic materials, such as mercury and PCB's, are beginning to appear. Conditions in the tributaries range from pristine to highly contaminated. Mountain tributary streams, such as the Harrison and Chilliwack, are in very good condition. Agricultural tributaries, such as the Salmon and Sumas, are in poorer condition because of depressed oxygen levels, high numbers of pathogens, and some increase in nutrient concentrations as well as in toxic materials. The Brunette basin in the heart of Greater Vancouver is contaminated by higher accumulations of toxic materials than is the main stem, and numbers of pathogens are high. Thus, if water quality conditions in the Lower Fraser are to be enhanced and preserved, discharges of pathogens and toxic materials must be controlled. In some tributaries it will also be necessary to control discharges of B.O.D. and nutrients.

Secondly, what are the sources of these pollutants? These are many and varied as illustrated by Figure 1. The most significant discharges directly to the water come from municipal treatment plants, industries, storm sewers and surface runoff. All contribute the pollutants of concern to some extent, and it cannot be said that any one is insignificant. Municipal treatment plants receive mixed wastes from a variety of domestic, commercial and industrial sources. Industries discharging directly to the Lower Fraser include fish processors,

POLLUTION PATHWAYS TO THE FRASER RIVER

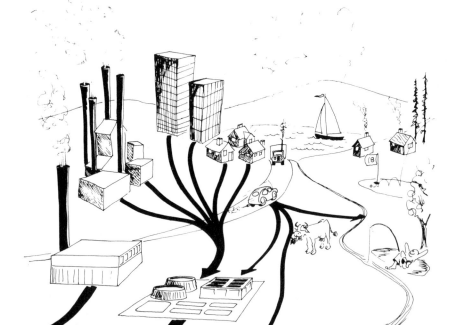

Figure 1

chemical manufacturers, saw mills, a distillery, paper mill, cement manufacturer and metal works. Urban runoff contains pollutants from materials put on the land and air pollutants that are precipitated or fall out from the atmosphere. Where sewer systems are combined, as in the City of Vancouver, pollutants in urban runoff are combined with the mixture of wastes in sanitary sewers. Where storm sewers are separate or the runoff is unsewered they enter the river directly. Thus the improvement and preservation of water quality in the Lower Fraser will depend on the control of discharges from this array of different sources.

The focus of this paper will be on control of these problem pollutants. The diversity of sources and pathways by which pollutants reach the Lower Fraser makes it necessary to consider diverse technologies and techniques for the control of discharges. The first part of this chapter therefore indicates how these control options must be analysed in terms of their effectiveness in controlling pollution and their cost. This is done firstly by considering in some detail one of the major municipal sources, the Annacis Island Sewage treatment plant. Then the effectiveness and costs of ways of controlling pollutant discharges from the other types of sources are considered in outline. The second part of this chapter suggests how procedures for implementing these techniques of pollution control might be strengthened. (For the detailed analyses underlying the first part see Dorcey *et al.* 1976a and the second part see Dorcey, 1976b and Dorcey *et al.* 1976c.)

TECHNOLOGIES AND TECHNIQUES OF CONTROL
The Annacis Island Sewage Treatment Plant

It is important to recognize that, although large, the Annacis plant is only one of the dischargers to the river. By volume its discharge is about 16 per cent of the total discharge to the Lower Fraser. The other G.V.R.D. sewage treatment plants at Iona and Lulu Islands contribute another 40 per cent, industries 39 per cent and municipalities upstream of Greater Vancouver only 5 per cent. If storm runoff is included it could double the total volume of discharges (Table 1). Annacis treats the sewage from the southern and eastern areas of the G.V.R.D. shown on the map. Prior to construction of this plant raw sewage was discharged at some 27 outfalls above Annacis Island and in the North Arm, White Rock's sewage was discharged to Boundary Bay, portions of Burnaby and Port Moody sewage were discharged to Burrard Inlet. It has recently been decided to divert the sewage from Ladner and South Delta to Annacis Island also (Figure 2).

Annacis, like Lulu and Iona, gives the sewage primary treatment and chlorination before discharge. Also, like Lulu, the effluent is dechlorinated. These processes disinfect the sewage and remove a portion of the toxic materials but a substantial proportion remains.

As required by Pollution Control Branch policy, all municipalities discharging to the Lower Fraser have provided for a minimum of primary treatment and chlorination. In anticipation of future requirements to upgrade their treatment, municipalities upstream of the G.V.R.D. either have already built or are building plants which will produce effluents of secondary quality. The G.V.R.D.,

Annacis Island Sewage Treatment Plant.   Fitch Cady

TABLE 1

DISCHARGES TO LOWER FRASER BY VOLUME

	Million Gallons/Day	Percent of Total
Annacis (a)	35	16
Iona (b)	83	39
Lulu (c)	3	1
Industries (d)	83	39
Upstream Municipalities (d)	10	5
	214	100
Runoff from GVRD (e)	85-220	

Notes:
a) Estimated average dry weather flow (dwf) when plant becomes fully operational in 1976. Present dwf capacity is 54 m.g.d.
b) Average daily flow in 1974. Present dwf capacity is 70 m.g.d.
c) Average daily flow in 1974. Present dwf capacity is 13 m.g.d.
d) Estimated from Provincial Pollution Control Branch permit data.
e) Based on estimates by Friesen, 1974.

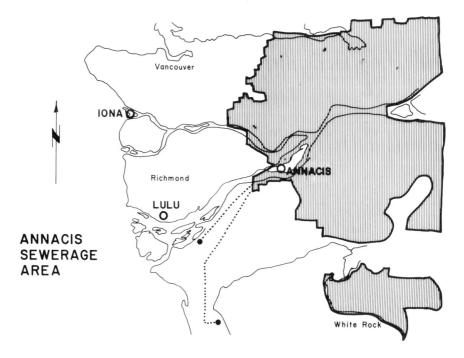

Figure 2

however, has appealed the decision of the Pollution Control Branch to require secondary treatment at Annacis and as a result, a technical committee was established under the provincial Environment and Land Use Committee Secretariat to analyse the options for upgrading the discharge. Westwater, together with representatives of federal and provincial agencies, is a member of this committee and has presented to it the analyses outlined below.

Since the water quality studies have indicated that the control of toxic materials requires the highest priority, attention has been focused on alternative ways of reducing the discharge of these materials from Annacis. Further, particular attention has been given to cumulative toxicants, such as heavy metals and chlorinated hydrocarbons, since toxicity due to degradable pollutants, such as ammonia and detergents, is unlikely to be significant even under the worst dilution conditions in the Lower Fraser.

Options for reducing pollutant discharges from Annacis

What are the choices for reducing further the pollutant discharge from Annacis? One is to control discharges at the source, so as to reduce and prevent some pollutants entering the sewers. Another is to build additional treatment facilities for increased pollutant removal. Let us consider the second one first, that is, the options for additional treatment. Figure 3 shows two different ap-

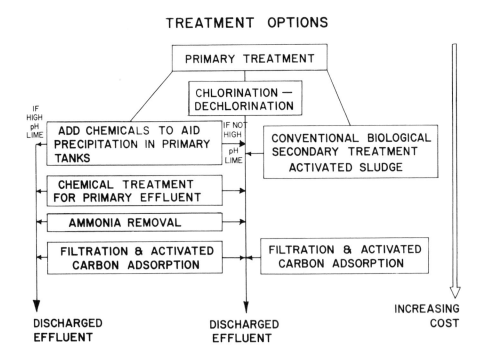

Figure 3

proaches that might be taken. On the right-hand side is shown the conventional approach to providing secondary treatment through the biological activated sludge process (see also Figure 4). If it were decided to reduce discharges even further by the addition of a tertiary process, filtration and activated carbon adsorption might be added to treat the secondary effluent. On the left-hand side of Figure 3 is shown an alternative approach, chemical treatment. This is a process with which there has so far been relatively little experience in North America. The chemicals used are usually lime or alum or, sometimes, ferric chloride. The first step would be to add chemicals to the existing primary settling tanks to aid precipitation and hence increase pollutant removal. As an alternative or, possibly, in addition, tanks could be added to provide chemical treatment of the primary effluent. Two tertiary processes might be considered to achieve higher removal. Firstly, since chemical treatment is relatively ineffective in removing ammonia, a process known as air-stripping might be used to lower ammonia concentrations in the chemical effluent. Secondly, filtration and activated carbon adsorption might be employed to provide even lower pollutant concentrations, just as in the case of the biological treatment option.

Unless chemical treatment with a high pH lime process is used, all of these options would require disinfection of the final effluent by chlorination and de-chlorination to remove the toxicity of residual chlorine.

The effectiveness of different treatment processes

How effective is the present primary treatment process in removing the pollutants of concern — pathogens and toxic materials? How much more effective are the options for additional treatment?

It is important to measure effectiveness in terms of both removal of individual pollutants and reduction in toxicity of the effluent. By considering the removal of individual pollutants it is possible to focus on those of particular concern. By using an acute toxicity bioassay — that is, a test which measures toxicity by the number of fish killed in a given time — valuable information can be obtained about the toxicity of an effluent which contains a mixture of pollutants. However, although no fish might die in such a test, concentrations can still be high enough to cause serious sublethal effects and through bioaccumulation become toxic to species higher up the food chain. It is for this reason that we must consider both measures of effectiveness.

Figure 5 shows the effectiveness of primary treatment, primary treatment with activated sludge and primary treatment with chemical treatment. On the vertical axis pollutant removal is shown as a percent of the raw sewage. On the horizontal axis are individual pollutants — the first three are B.O.D., ammonia and MBAS (methylene blue active substances, which include such materials as detergents). These three pollutants can contribute very significantly to the acute toxicity of the effluent but, since they are biodegradable, their toxicity will likely decrease rapidly in the Fraser. The other pollutants are heavy metals and chlorinated hydrocarbons which are cumulative toxicants and hence can cause chronic toxicity even though they may not cause acute toxicity in the effluent.

1. PRESENT PRIMARY PLANT AT ANNACIS

2. PRIMARY & BIOLOGICAL SECONDARY

3. PRIMARY & BIOLOGICAL SECONDARY & TERTIARY

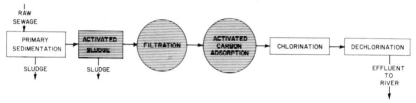

4. CHEMICAL PRIMARY

5. PRIMARY & CHEMICAL TREATMENT

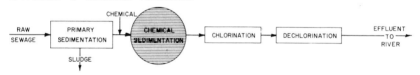

6. CHEMICAL PRIMARY & AMMONIA REMOVAL

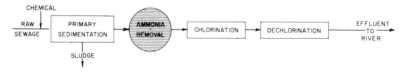

7. CHEMICAL PRIMARY & FILTRATION & ACTIVATED CARBON ADSORPTION

Figure 4   Combinations of Treatment Options.

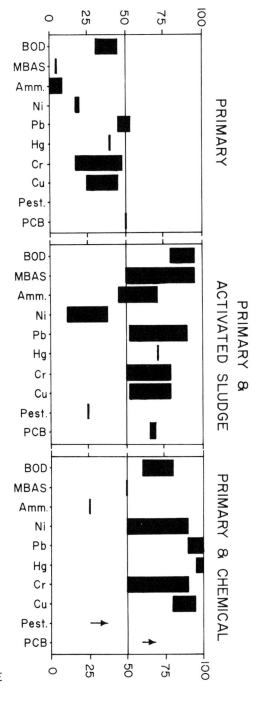

PERCENT REMOVAL
FROM RAW SEWAGE

Figure 5   Treatment Effectiveness   Dorcey *et al.*, 1976a.

These performance data are based on experience reported in the literature. The length of the bar indicates the range of performance that has been reported. Because of the relatively recent emergence of concern for these toxicants the performance data for all three processes are fragmentary. This range therefore does not always indicate the range of average performance between plants. Where there is only a line only one number has been found. However, although not necessarily shown by this data, it is important to remember that the performance of any plant is likely to vary substantially over time and that there will be substantial variation between the average performance of different plants using the same process. This is a result of many factors, in particular, changes in pollutant concentration in the raw waste, overloading of the plant, variations in operation and poor management. Nevertheless important conclusions can be drawn from this data:

1. Primary treatment removes a small but significant amount, at least 25% of most pollutants and as much as 50% for a few of them. The notable exceptions are MBAS, ammonia and nickel.

2. The addition of either activated sludge or chemical treatment increases the removal of most pollutants to more than 50% — the exceptions being, in the case of activated sludge, nickel and pesticides, and in the case of chemical treatment, ammonia and possibly pesticides.

3. Figure 6 shows more clearly a comparison of the effectiveness of the activated sludge and chemical processes on a pollutant-by-pollutant basis. It indicates

   a) A well operated activated sludge plant will be more effective in removing the degradable pollutants — B.O.D., ammonia and MBAS.

   b) A chemical treatment plant can be more effective in removing heavy metals and, although only data for treating industrial wastes have been found, it is thought likely that chemical treatment will be more effective than activated sludge in removing pesticides and PCB's. This is indicated by the arrows.

4. The third column from the left shows that ammonia removal could be increased to more than 90% if the air-stripping process is added along with the chemical plant.

5. Although not shown here, if a tertiary process involving filtration and activated carbon adsorption were added to either biological or chemical treatment, very high levels of reduction, in most cases in excess of 90%, can be achieved.

How do these processes compare in their reduction of acute toxicity? Despite the importance of this measure of effectiveness only one study has been found which compares the toxicity reduction of these treatment processes. Very great care must be taken in generalizing from this study to the Annacis situation because it is not known how the conclusions might be altered by sewage containing different mixtures of pollutants, by variations in the basic treatment processes considered and by substituting salmonids for the golden shiners used in these bioassays. The addition of chemical treatment reduced the acute toxicity

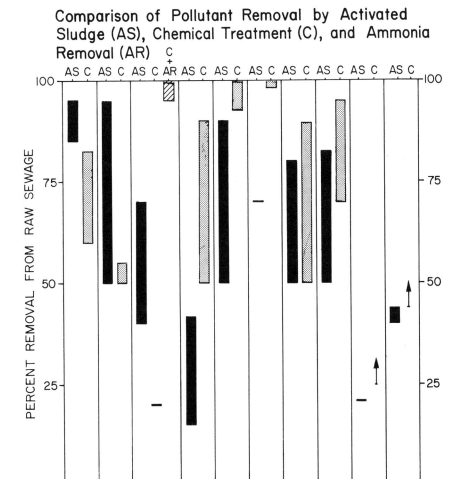

Figure 6

of primary effluent by 40%, the further addition of ammonia removal increased the toxicity removal to 65% and the further addition of activated carbon adsorption increased toxicity removal to 75%. Biological treatment also reduced the acute toxicity of primary effluent by 75% (Figure 7). Since it was estimated that 67% of the acute toxicity of the primary effluent was due to ammonia and MBAS, these results are consistent with what would be expected because of the greater effectiveness of activated sludge in removing these biodegradable pollutants. Although other toxic materials, including heavy metals, were detected in the primary effluent, their removal was unfortunately not measured and so it was not possible to estimate how much their toxicity was reduced.

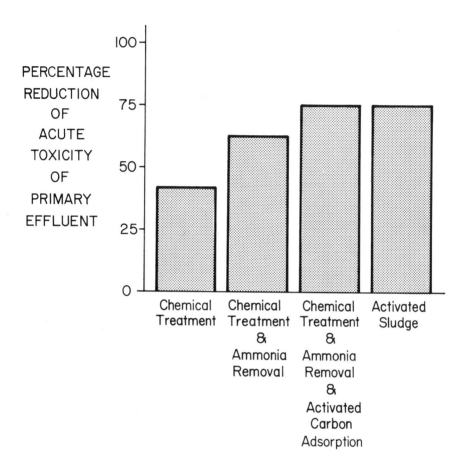

Figure 7   Esvelt *et al.*, 1973.

California study of acute toxicity reduction by additions to primary plant using Golden Shiners.

In brief then, it would appear that either biological or chemical treatment can significantly increase pollutant removal and toxicity reduction, that biological treatment is more effective in removing the biodegradable pollutants — B.O.D., ammonia and MBAS — and chemical treatment is more effective in removing cumulative toxicants. The further addition of ammonia removal, filtration and activated carbon adsorption could produce high levels of reduction for all pollutants. In choosing between the biological and chemical treatment options much will depend on the flow of the waters into which the wastes are to be discharged. In a river such as the Fraser, any effluent toxicity from ammonia and MBAS will likely be reduced very rapidly through degradation and dilution even under the worst dilution conditions. It seems therefore that in the Fraser more importance should be given to effectiveness in removing cumulative pollutants and, thus, to chemical treatment.

The cost of different treatment processes

However to make a choice between these alternatives it is not only necessary to know their effectiveness but also their costs.

Figure 8 shows the two different approaches to adding greater treatment at Annacis. The numbers in the boxes are estimates of the costs of each process in cents per thousand gallons treated. The estimates are based on literature data which give a good indication of relative process costs but may not reflect precisely the costs that would be incurred if the facilities were built at Annacis. The costs are in 1975 dollars, they include amortization of capital, and operation and maintenance costs, but have not accounted for the Federal or Provincial subsidies that would be available.

The present primary plant costs about 9 cents per thousand gallons and chlorination-dechlorination adds one and one half cents to this. The addition of activated sludge at 11 cents/1,000 gallons would more than double present costs

TREATMENT COSTS FOR ANNACIS ISLAND S.T.P. IN CENTS/1000 GALLONS

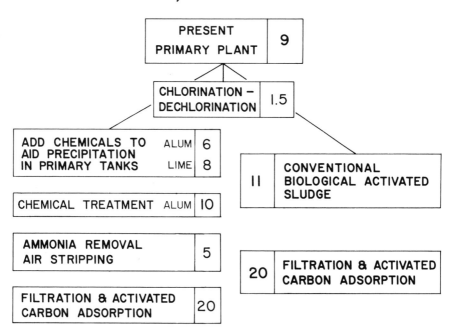

Figure 8   Dorcey *et al.*, 1976a.

but both the chemical options might be cheaper — if alum is added in the present primary plant, only 6 cents/1,000 gallons, or if lime is added, 8 cents/1,000 gallons, and if full chemical treatment with alum is provided, 10 cents/1,000 gallons, possibly a little less than activated sludge. Ammonia removal by air stripping might be added to a chemical process for 5 cents/1,000 gallons. Under either approach tertiary treatment by filtration and activated carbon at 20 cents/1,000 gallons might cost as much again as primary and secondary treatment combined.

These costs do not, however, include the costs of sludge processing and disposal. It is too often forgotten that in removing pollutants, treatment plants produce a sludge, which contains the heavy metals and chlorinated hydro-carbons removed in treatment and that, if a secondary treatment process is added, the quantity of sludge is at least doubled. If the sludge contains substantial quantities of toxic materials it cannot be safely incinerated without scrubbing and treating the stack gases or put on the land without preparing the site to prevent leaching. Otherwise the toxic materials will enter the waterway eventually either as fall-out or runoff.

The sludge from the present primary plant is digested and then lagooned beside the plant. The Annacis site is however too small to allow for long-term sludge disposal unless it is incinerated. The option that has been considered for long-term off-site disposal is lagooning of mature sludge on Burns Bog by piping the digested sludge under the river to the south shore. The costs of sludge processing and disposal are estimated to be between 4 and 6 cents per 1,000 gallons of treated sewage. Land disposal in Burns Bog is slightly cheaper than incineration and the processes generating less sludge, for example alum treatment as opposed to lime treatment, are at the lower end of this cost range.

Figure 9 indicates the total costs of both treatment and sludge disposal. With the present primary plant and lagooning of the sludge on Annacis Island it costs 10 cents/1,000 gallons treated or about $7 a year for each person served. Assuming the sludge is put on the land in Burns Bog the total cost of various combinations of additional treatment can be compared with the present costs. At $12 a year per person, adding alum in the present primary plant would be cheaper than adding lime. If the primary effluent were given chemical treatment with alum the annual cost per person would increase to $16. The addition of an activated sludge plant, on the other hand, would cost only slightly more, less than a dollar, than alum treatment. If ammonia were removed from the effluent of an alum primary plant, costs would rise to $19 a year per person or if filtration and activated carbon were added to the alum primary plant total costs would reach $26 per person per year. If the cost of chlorination and dechlorination is included 1.5 cents/1,000 gallons should be added to the total cost of each of these combinations of treatment.

In summary then, if more money is to be invested in additional treatment at Annacis, which investments might be most effective in improving water quality conditions? The analyses described suggest the following conclusions (Figure 10):

ANNACIS COST OF TREATMENT AND
SLUDGE DISPOSAL ON BURNS BOG

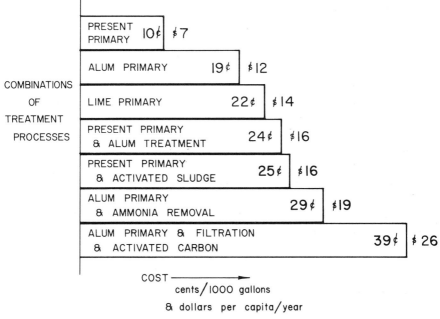

Figure 9   Dorcey *et al.*, 1976a.

COST-EFFECTIVENESS OF TREATMENT AT ANNACIS STP

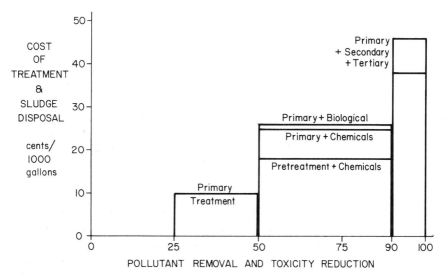

Figure 10   Dorcey *et al.*, 1976.

1. The addition of alum in the present primary plant would increase costs about 90 - 120% and increase pollutant removals substantially, although not as much as either of the two secondary processes.
2. Both chemical treatment processes might be cheaper than activated sludge and more effective in removing the toxic pollutants of concern in the Lower Fraser.
3. The addition of secondary and tertiary treatment will at least quadruple costs but can achieve very high levels of removal.

In deciding what course to pursue several factors should be considered. First, because of the limited municipal experience with chemical treatment and the removal of toxic materials by activated sludge, it would be advisable to experiment with pilot plants to determine more precisely the effectiveness of these options before deciding whether or not to adopt either of them. Second, it is important to bear in mind that the addition of a tertiary treatment stage to primary and secondary treatment processes nearly doubles the costs and yet achieves only a modest increase in the reduction of toxic discharges. Third, and of major significance, removal of toxic materials in a treatment plant results in their accumulation in the sludge which must be disposed of in the environment in some way. If toxic materials can be removed at their source this problem would be overcome.

Source Control in Sewers

It is now evident that a source control programme is not simply an alternative way of reducing discharges from Annacis but possibly the only way of lowering concentrations of toxic materials in sludges. This of course applies not only to Annacis, which I have described in some detail for illustrative purposes, but also to the plants at Iona and Lulu. Source control can also in some cases be more effective and less costly than additional treatment at the municipal plant. By controlling the discharges from a few industries, substantial reductions in concentrations and loads of toxic materials in sewers can be achieved.

The source control problem and opportunity is well illustrated by the electro-plating industry. All except 6 of more than 25 firms in the Greater Vancouver metal finishing industry discharge to the sewers. In Chapter 3, Ken Hall has described the very much higher concentrations of heavy metals in the sewers draining industrial areas which include electroplating plants. For these areas it was estimated that on a per capita basis the load of some trace metals, for example nickel, could be as much as 100 times the load from urban-industrial areas without plating plants. Thus controlling discharges from platers could substantially reduce peak concentrations and total loads of metals coming into treatment plants. Besides well developed treatment technology, there are very significant opportunities in this industry to prevent the generation of wastes; these include substituting non-toxic organic chemicals for cyanide in process solutions, changing processes to use lower concentrations of plating solutions, particularly chromium, designing dipping processes to reduce drag-out from plating tanks, economizing on rinse water to avoid large volumes of very dilute

Vancouver area electroplating operation.   Doug Miller

waste, building floor drains to capture and keep separate spills of different plating solutions and, perhaps most significant of all, instituting good "house-keeping" practices to avoid spills and equipment failure such as tank and drain leaks.

Experience with source control programmes has shown that they can be most effective. For example, in Los Angeles mercury in sewers was reduced from 33 pounds a day to 7 pounds a day by persuading a large variety of industries to use other materials (Tillman et al., 1973). It has also been found that the adminis-tration of such programmes need not be unduly expensive and that sewer charge schemes can be designed such that the programme is self-financing (Demakeas, 1974. Seagraves, 1973). The Greater Vancouver Sewerage and Drainage District has estimated that an initial programme for Greater Vancouver might cost $300,000 per year, that is, less than one half of one dollar per year per person served by the Iona, Lulu and Annacis plants. Hence source control can be very effective and yet need not be very costly.

The Other Sources

The municipal treatment plants are only one of three major groups of sources discharging directly to the Lower Fraser, the others being industry and runoff. These too must be analysed just as the municipal sources to determine the effectiveness and costs of ways of preventing the generation of pollutants and treating wastes. What appear to be the more cost-effective control options for each of these sources are very briefly indicated below.

Industries

Like the electroplater on the municipal sewers, industrial wastes can in general be controlled by preventing their generation and processing the wastes produced before they are discharged into the environment. The generation of wastes can be avoided by changing the raw materials used, altering the production process, redesigning the product manufactured and by recycling production materials. Once the wastes are produced, discharges can be controlled by producing by-products, by treatment and by transporting them for disposal elsewhere. The existence of these options and their relative cost-effectiveness will vary greatly between industries, between firms within any one industry and between locations. Two important conclusions can, however, be drawn from experience in controlling industrial waste discharges in North America and Europe:

1. There is no industry for which technology does not exist for processing its waste to produce a high quality effluent. However, present technology for doing this may be very costly.
2. It has frequently been found that in-plant process changes are cheaper than on-site treatment, particularly if changes are made when the plant is being designed. Some firms have even increased their profits as a result of process changes that were originally made for controlling the generation of wastes.

This suggests that for industries of Greater Vancouver and the Lower Fraser it would be important to consider carefully the cost-effectiveness of the non-treatment alternatives for reducing discharges. In electroplating plants this means examining the opportunities for substitution of non-toxic chemicals for cyanide. In fish processing plants there are opportunities for producing animal feed and recovering oil from the wastes. In refineries, sulphur and ammonia can be recovered to keep them out of process waste waters and spent caustics can be sold to other producers. For example, sulphide spent caustics can be used by paper mills and phenolic spent caustics can be used to produce cresylic acid, which is used in making synthetic resins and antiseptics.

Runoff

The control of the pathogens and toxic materials in runoff poses the most difficult problems in water quality management, especially in an urban industrial region. It will be necessary to devote a great deal of study and investigation to these problems over a relatively long period before fully satisfactory control measures can be devised. I will review rather briefly some of the steps that can be taken (Figure 11).

First, it is evident that the production and distribution of some toxic materials should be carefully controlled. This usually can best be done at the point of production. Some of the measures undertaken today include restricting the sale of PCB's, the banning of some forms of pesticides, and the movement to eliminate the use of lead in gasoline. Here in the Lower Fraser it is important to be attentive to the identification of toxic materials that can best be controlled at

CONTROLLING   RUNOFF

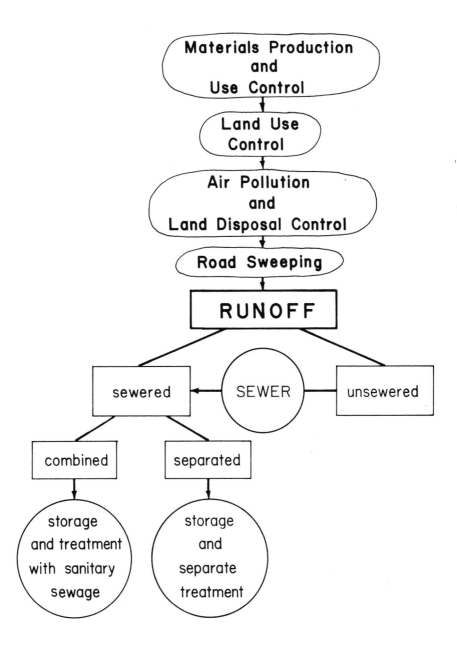

Figure 11

the source and to make representation to the federal government to utilize its authority under the recently enacted environmental contaminants legislation to control the production and distribution of such pollutants.

Second, a wide range of measures to reduce the quantities of contaminants from runoff require investigation and analysis. These include land use controls, regulation of pollutants in air and land disposal, improved sweeping of roads in some areas and the possibility of using some inexpensive form of treatment for runoff collected in storm sewers.

— If soils and drainage are taken into account in developing land use controls, contamination of runoff can be avoided — for example, by prohibiting septic tank disposal on gravelly soils, preserving green belts along stream banks to filter runoff, designing developments so that storm water infiltration into the soil is maximized and adequate storm drainage systems constructed to carry the increased flows.

— Air pollutants are precipitated and fall-out onto the land, from where they enter runoff. Toxic materials disposed of in land fills can leach out and enter runoff. Consequently effective air pollution and solid waste management policies should be designed to keep toxic materials, such as mercury, lead and pesticides, out of runoff.

— Cleaning the roads with new vacuum sweepers will prevent contaminated street sediments from entering stream runoff. In Chapter 3, Ken Hall described the accumulation of heavy metals and chlorinated hydrocarbons found in Vancouver street sediments, particularly in the fine sediments. Studies in the U.S. have found that whilst conventional brush sweepers remove only 15% of the fine sediments, high levels of removal can be achieved with vacuum sweepers (Sartor et al., 1972).

— Unsewered runoff can always be sewered and treated, but the costs of each of these are great. Furthermore, where runoff is already sewered in a combined system, as in the drainage to the Iona plant from Vancouver, problems are created that call for special attention. Specifically, during rainstorms the flow through the Iona sewage treatment plant increases and its efficiency is reduced. During large storms some of the combined sanitary and storm sewage by-passes the plant and hence receives no treatment. The efficiency of treatment can be increased and storm runoff treated if a means is provided to store temporarily the peak flows. The two major opportunities for storage are lagooning adjacent to the plant and the development of a computerized system for utilizing the storage available in the actual collection pipes, as has been done in Seattle and several other U.S. cities (Leiser, 1974). An alternative approach is to alter the combined system so that only the first flush of the storm, which contains the higher concentrations of pollutants, is carried to the plant and subsequent storm flows are diverted. Just what treatment might be most appropriate for this combined sewage must be analyzed as has been described for Annacis. The higher and more variable flows that occur in a combined sanitary and storm sewage plant such as Iona make it particularly important to compare chemical treatment with activated sludge and, in the

Urban runoff is a major source of toxic materials.   Fitch Cady

case of Iona where there is more land available, with another option for biological secondary treatment, namely high-rate trickling filtration.

Although the opportunities for controlling pollutants in runoff have been described only briefly, it is obvious why it is suggested that these may pose the most difficult problems in water quality management.

A Regional Toxic Waste Facility

There is one other type of control that must be considered, one that might be used in controlling the discharges of toxic materials from municipal sewers, industry and runoff, and one that could be critical to the preservation of environmental quality and public health. This is a regional facility for the reclamation, treatment and disposal of toxic materials. Reclamation of raw materials may not be feasible on-site, particularly for smaller plants, but be feasible if done by a regional facility serving a number of waste producers. This could apply to waste solvents, used lubricating oils and heavy metals in electroplating plant sludges. Often industries have toxic wastes for which they have no safe means of disposal — these may be sludges from their treatment process, spoilt chemicals or wastes which cannot be treated on-site because of the lack of space or the specialized technology required. A regional facility could be built to reclaim materials and to give non-reclaimable toxic materials appropriate treatment for safe disposal.

Experience in the United States has shown that with some ingenuity one firm's wastes may be combined with another's to produce a product that yet another will buy. Table 2 shows just some of the materials that have been reclaimed and products that have been produced from a variety of wastes at one plant near Seattle. Copper, zinc, mercury, cyanide, oil and solvents have all been reclaimed from wastes. By combining reclaimed materials and wastes various new products have been made. Chromium rinse water from platers has been combined with lead batteries to produce lead chromate for yellow highway paint. Waste zinc from galvanizing plants has been the basis for producing zinc oxide for paint manufacturers, fire retardant and fertilizers for onions, hops and beans. Flue dust from a steel mill has been the basis for producing a moss killer, lawn fertilizer and ferric chloride for sewage treatment plants. Finally, for chicken feathers — a difficult disposal problem even if they are not toxic. A process was developed to break-down the protein chain so that the feathers could be fed back to the chickens.

A regional facility should therefore emphasize reclamation and the production of by-products. Treatment for safe disposal would only be used if the other two options are not feasible. Through reclamation valuable materials can be conserved and the rate of increase of the total quantity of toxic materials in use can be reduced. Toxic wastes can be used in the manufacture of non-polluting by-products and this can be more economical than their treatment and disposal.

Greater Vancouver does not at present have a facility such as this although some of its toxic wastes are going to various plants in Washington State. As control over toxic materials presently going into the sewers, the atmosphere and

TABLE 2

REGIONAL FACILITY

WASTE	RECLAIMED MATERIAL
Printed Circuit Board Solution	Copper
Waste Zinc Sludge	Zinc
Mercury Batteries	Mercury
Cyanide Baths	Cyanide
Waste Oils	Oil
Waste Solvents	Solvents

WASTE	NEW PRODUCT
Chromium Rinse Water & Lead Batteries	Yellow Highway Paint
Waste Zinc from Galvanizers	Paint Fire Retardant Fertilizer (onions, hops, beans)
Steel Mill Flue Dust	Moss Killer Lawn Fertilizer Sewage Treatment Chemical
Chicken Feathers	Chicken Feed

Source: Western Processing Co. Inc. 1975

solid waste sites becomes more stringent, it will increasingly be necessary to have some place to which pollution control agencies can direct toxic wastes. Careful consideration should therefore be given as to how to provide the services of such a facility in Greater Vancouver. This could be through the development of a processing facility for the region or merely the establishment of a regional collection facility which utilized processing plants elsewhere, perhaps in Washington State.

The very difficult task facing pollution control agencies in the Lower Fraser is now apparent. People want controls to be effective and yet unlimited amounts of money cannot be invested in pollution control. It is, therefore, critical that agencies have the capability to analyse the cost-effectiveness of controlling discharges from runoff, municipal sewers and industry. Further, that they be able to identify what combination of controls at these different sources would be most effective if people are willing to spend $10, $50 or $100 million a year. With this information a more informed judgement can be made as to how much to spend to improve water quality conditions and how best it might be spent to lower the probability of future toxicity problems developing.

POLICY IMPLEMENTATION

Until now pollution control policies have been concerned with sewage and direct industrial discharges to the river. If, as the analyses indicate, it is necessary to implement other types of control, will new legislation be required? All the types of control that have been discussed could be implemented under existing legislation (Table 3). Sewage treatment and the control of direct industrial discharges to the river through in-plant process changes and treatment are already implemented through the permit system under the provincial Pollution Control Act. The collection, storage and treatment of run-off could also be implemented under this act. Municipal by-laws already exist for regulating discharges into their sewers. Land use controls could be implemented through municipal and regional zoning regulation. And, the new Federal Environmental Contaminants Act provides the means for implementing any desired controls over the production and use of materials.

The effective implementation of pollution control policies however depends on factors other than legislative authority alone. Three factors that appear to be of critical importance are considered here:

    a) the information provided by waste producers in applying for a discharge permit

TABLE 3

TYPE OF CONTROL	LEGISLATIVE AUTHORITY
1. Municipal Sewage Treatment	Permit under provincial Pollution Control Act
2. Industry — Treatment and in-plant changes	,,
3. Runoff — Collection, storage, treatment	,,
4. Discharge into sewers	Municipal and Regional By-laws
5. Runoff — Land Use Controls	Municipal and Regional Zoning Regulations
6. Toxic Materials — Production and use	Federal Environmental Contaminants Act

b) the capability of pollution control agencies to assess the costs and effectiveness of controlling discharges from various sources, and

c) the incentives available to pollution control agencies to influence the behaviour of waste dischargers.

Information from Applicants to Discharge Wastes

In Chapter 7, Mark Sproule-Jones and Ken Peterson indicate the central role of the Pollution Control Branch permit process in the implementation of pollution control in the Lower Fraser. A firm wishing to discharge its wastes into the river fills out an application, indicating the location of the outfall and characteristics of the proposed discharge. This application is then reviewed by the Branch, other governmental agencies, including the federal Fisheries Service and Environmental Protection Service, and various public interest groups, such as the B.C. Wildlife Federation and SPEC. After taking into account review comments, the Branch either rejects the application or issues a permit to discharge as long as specific conditions are met.

There are several weaknesses that stem from the present application process. Firstly, the information contained on permit applications frequently is not adequate for the Branch or other reviewers to assess the impact of a discharge. Ken Hall, in Chapter 3 on the sources of pollution, explained that we were unable to assess the contribution of industries to the discharge of toxic materials because of the lack of data. Also, since the total quantity of toxic materials used by a producer is not accounted for, the impact of the activity on the air, land and water cannot be assessed nor can problems of shifting pollutants from the water to the land or air be anticipated. Secondly, the waste producer is very well able, in some ways better able than pollution control agencies, to identify opportunities to control his discharge and estimate their cost but this type of information is presently not included in the application. Thirdly, since the applicant is not required to assess the impact of his proposed discharge, important information for making such an assessment is omitted and each of the reviewers has to make his own assessment. Because they lack the necessary resources and expertise, some reviewers are unable to assess how their interests will be affected.

By making changes in the information required from permit applicants it is more likely that necessary questions will be asked and given adequate consideration before a discharge is permitted. Four changes might be made in implementation procedures to begin to move in this direction.

1. Applicants for a Pollution Control Branch permit would be required to submit details of the materials used on-site and flow and concentration data on the proportions of toxicants which go into the final product, sewers, incineration and solid waste disposal. Also required would be a cost-effectiveness analysis of ways to reduce discharges into the environment. To avoid unnecessary expense only this basic information might be required in the initial application; then, if it is found that the application is

for a discharge into a particularly sensitive receiving water or that toxic materials are being used, more detailed impact analyses might be required.

2. Non-domestic dischargers into a municipal sewer would be required to obtain a permit from the Greater Vancouver Sewerage and Drainage District. The application would require the same materials balance data as the discharger to the river. Since there are a very large number of potential permittees in the G.V.R.D., its introduction would be staged with the introduction of a source control programme and begin with the most problematic sources, such as the metal finishing industry.

3. Land developers would be required to demonstrate to municipal and regional authorities how storm runoff would be collected and its effect on the drainage system.

4. Manufacturers of new chemicals would be required to demonstrate that their products will not cause environmental hazards. If reasonable doubt remains, it would be necessary to provide information on the benefits from use of the material and the costs to society if it is not used. Such an approach could be taken under the new Environmental Contaminants Act.

Information Generation by Pollution Control Agencies

In Chapter 7 it is concluded that management agencies do not generate adequate information to control pollution effectively in the Lower Fraser. Other papers in this volume have indicated the type of comprehensive information required about the damages caused by waste discharges, the sources of pollutants and the cost-effectiveness of control techniques. Unless pollution control agencies have comprehensive information about water quality conditions and the capability to estimate the impact of allowing new discharges, informed judgements cannot be made on permit applications. Also, unless these agencies are able to assess the cost and effectiveness of the ways of controlling discharges they will be in a very weak position in negotiating with waste producers. It is therefore essential to provide, within the network of agencies responsible for pollution control, the capability both to generate comprehensive information on the Fraser system and assess critically the information from applications to discharge wastes.

If applications for a Pollution Control Branch permit provide the materials balance data suggested above then the Branch should be able to make an initial assessment of the impact of the proposed discharge. Where the Branch feels this assessment is not adequate because of the type or size or location of the discharge, the applicant should be required to undertake specific studies to provide the necessary data. Together with the information provided on ways of reducing the discharge, the Branch could indicate what waste management facilities would be required to reduce environmental impacts to the level it considers necessary. Other government agencies and the public would then be asked to review three things (i) the information on the application, (ii) the initial impact assessment and (iii) the waste management practices proposed for reducing the impact of the discharge. By providing reviewers with this specific information they will all be much better able than under present procedures to judge how the proposed discharge will affect their interests and to comment constructively on the proposed permit. These changes will thus greatly improve participation in the permit granting process and hence strengthen the implementation of pollution control.

If this approach is extended to the regulation of land use and the production of new chemicals, it likewise implies providing the capability to assess critically the information provided by the developer.

The Incentive to Control Pollution

The effectiveness of pollution control implementation will also depend on a third factor, that is, the incentive that agencies can give to waste dischargers to comply with regulations, to consider the costs of waste discharge and to develop non-polluting technologies. At present, there is quite a variety of incentive mechanisms available to pollution control agencies. Some of these mechanisms rely on the threat of prosecution and fines, others on subsidies to reduce the costs of pollution control.

Compliance with permits issued under the provincial Pollution Control Act, with regulations issued under the federal Fisheries Act and with regulations established in sewer by-laws is induced by the threat of prosecution and fines. The usefulness of the incentives provided by these provisions is, however, limited because of the expense, delay and difficulty of successful prosecution. It is largely for these reasons that relatively few dischargers have been prosecuted. With few examples of successful prosecution, the incentive effects of these mechanisms are limited.

Subsidies are available to both municipalities and industries to reduce the cost of pollution control. Municipalities can obtain loans up to two-thirds of the cost of constructing sewage collection and treatment facilities from the federal Central Mortgage and Housing Corporation. Upon completion of the project 25% of the principal and accrued interest is forgiven. Grants can also be obtained under the provincial Sewerage Facilities Assistance Act for 75% of the costs of the annual debt charge for sewerage facilities over a 3 mill levy. Industries can reduce the costs of pollution control by deducting them in the calculation of their corporate income tax; for large firms this will about halve their costs. Although these subsidies are very substantial they do not have significant incentive effects because they are not integrated into pollution control. If subsidies were made conditional on compliance with the requirements of pollution control agencies they might have some influence on the behaviour of the waste producer.

Thus it would appear that the implementation of pollution control in the Lower Fraser might be made more effective by providing agencies with more convenient and flexible incentive mechanisms. Two steps might be taken to do this:

1. A charge on discharges permitted by the Pollution Control Branch. The charge would be two-part to reflect both the volume of the discharge and the concentrations of pollutants in it. If the permit conditions were not

TABLE 4

CHARGE FORMULA

ANNUAL COST = PRICE x VOLUME   if no violation
 ($/year)   (c/gallon) (gallons/year)

PLUS if there is a violation

$$\text{PENALTY} \quad x \quad \frac{\text{MEASURED VOLUME}}{\text{PERMITTED VOLUME}} \quad x \quad \frac{\text{MEASURED QUALITY}}{\text{PERMITTED QUALITY}}$$

exceeded the annual charge would be based solely on the volume discharged. If either the permitted volume or the permitted quality characteristics of the effluent were exceeded then there would be an additional annual charge, equal to a penalty fee multiplied by a factor to reflect the extent of the violation (Table 4). The basic charge could be set to cover the administrative costs of implementing pollution control, including monitoring and enforcement, and some of the costs of research into damages caused by waste discharges. It might also include a small royalty for use of the provincial water resource. Any excess revenue would go into general revenue.

2. A sewer surcharge: A surcharge would be levied on non-domestic discharges to the sewers. This charge would also be two-part. The basic charge would be based on volume as measured by the metered water supply. Any violation of the permitted volume or quality would result in an additional charge proportional to the violation. The basic charge could be set to cover the costs of the source control programme plus a portion of the costs of treating the non-domestic wastes.

If these two charge schemes were used in implementing pollution control there would be an ongoing incentive to waste producers to find less costly and more effective control techniques. Also the existence of an automatic penalty could provide a very effective incentive to comply with regulations.

The suggested improvements for information would undoubtedly increase the pollution control costs of both the waste discharger and management agencies. However, the use of these charge schemes would not be costly to administer if they were based on information that would have to be collected in any event for monitoring and enforcement. But, obviously, they could increase the costs of dischargers who pay the charge. Hence, just as more effective technology will be costly, so will more effective implementation of pollution control policies.

SUMMARY AND CONCLUSIONS

Yesterday the policies necessary for controlling pollution seemed simple and obvious, today they appear complex and uncertain. We used to think that if only we could get treatment plants on the end of municipal and industrial sewers, problems would be solved, because BOD, suspended solids and pathogens would be removed. Then, as eutrophication problems became more common, we thought nutrients should also be removed. Although runoff was recognized to be a source of these nutrients, we tended to neglect it because we just could not come to grips with the difficulties of controlling non-point sources. Recently, following major tragedies in other parts of the world, we have become alarmed about pesticides and heavy metals. Today, these are thought to be only two of many groups of toxic materials that in their use by man threaten his health and the ecosystem. It is becoming increasingly evident that we cannot afford to neglect runoff as a source of toxic materials. There are now concerns with the toxic effects of many different materials, and as analytical techniques are developed these concerns seem to develop for even lower concentrations. In addition it has been recognized that no pathway to the aquatic environment can be neglected, nor can the control of toxic materials in the water be separated from their control on the land and in the atmosphere.

It is now evident that diverse control techniques and positive policies will be necessary if toxicity problems are to be avoided. The more cost-effective policies appear to be those that prevent the generation of the toxic material or waste. Where this is not possible, reclamation of raw materials or manufacture of by-products can often be more efficient than treatment. Policies for controlling toxic materials must be positive, or else there is a very real risk that the solution of a water pollution problem could be at the cost of some very much greater health hazard. It is not sufficient to prohibit a toxic material in a municipal or industrial sewer; as long as that waste continues to be generated it must also be established where and how it can be disposed of.

If these kinds of controls are to be implemented effectively, management agencies must be capable of negotiating with waste dischargers from a position of strength. This implies that they must have the capability to generate information about the damages from waste discharges, analyse the cost-effectiveness of control techniques and induce dischargers to comply with regulations. Three steps which might be taken to strengthen the implementation of pollution control have been suggested: firstly, put the initial responsibility on the waste discharger to establish the impact of his activities, secondly, provide management agencies with the capability to evaluate the discharger's information and analyse his impact on other uses of the resource and, thirdly, provide pollution control agencies with economic incentives that they can use to influence the behaviour of waste dischargers.

REFERENCES
Demakeas, J. 1974. Effluent charges in Canada. Paper presented at O.E.C.D. Conference.

Dorcey, A.H.J.; Bethell, G.; and Robinson, G. 1976a. *Controlling the toxicity of municipal wastewaters: technologies and policies for the Lower Fraser.* Westwater Research Centre, University of British Columbia, Vancouver. (In preparation).

Dorcey, A.H.J. 1976b. Policy Mechanisms for water quality management in a metropolitan area: Greater Vancouver and the Fraser Estuary, in *The Practical Application of Economic Incentives to the Control of Pollution: The Case of British Columbia*, ed. James Stephenson, University of British Columbia Press Vancouver. (In press).

———. 1976c. *The design of regulations and economic incentives for pollution control in the Lower Fraser.* Westwater Research Centre, University of British Columbia, Vancouver. (In preparation).

Esvelt, L.A.; Kaufman, W.J.; and Selleck, R.E. 1973. Toxicity assessment of treated municipal wastewaters. *Journal Water Pollution Control Federation* 45(7):1558-1572.

Friesen, K. 1974. An estimation of runoff into the Fraser River from the Greater Vancouver Regional District. Westwater Research Centre, University of British Columbia, Vancouver.

Leiser, C.P. 1974. *Computer management of a combined sewer system.* Environmental Protection Technology Series. EPA 670/2-74-022. Environmental Protection Agency, Washington, U.S.

Sartor, J.D., and Boyd, G.B. 1972. *Water pollution aspects of street surface contaminants.* Environmental Protection Technology Series. EPA-R2-72-081. Environmental Protection Agency, Washington, U.S.

Seagraves, J.A. 1973. Industrial wastes charges. Paper presented at the 1973 National Water Resources Engineering meeting, American Society of Civil Engineers, January 1973.

Tillman, D.C., and Bargman, R.D. 1973. *Report on waste discharges to the ocean.* Department of Public Works, Los Angeles.

Western Processing Co. Inc. 1975. Paper presented at a Public Meeting held by the U.S. Environmental Protection Agency, San Francisco, 11 December, 1975.

7

Pollution Control
in the Lower Fraser:
Who's in Charge?

by Mark H. Sproule-Jones and Kenneth G. Peterson

Pollution and pollution control involve social as well as physical and biological processes. The concentration of population and industry in a region has many consequences for the natural environment: some are inevitable and unavoidable, others can be prevented or ameliorated. Social processes alter the natural environment, and attempts to understand how the environment is being altered and how these changes can be controlled are also social processes. The pollutants that enter the environment, the studies and tests done to determine their presence and their effects and the procedures established for eliminating, controlling or rendering them innocuous are all the result of human decision-making processes. To ask who is in charge of pollution control in the Lower Fraser is fundamentally to ask how these decision-making processes work.

We stress these points here in our introductory remarks because none of these processes can be excluded from scrutiny in trying to understand how pollution control works in the Lower Fraser. We cannot simply look at the application of a law or a set of laws or at the functions of one or two agencies charged with the responsibility of pollution control. These are important. Indeed they play a central role in what we call the *water quality provision system,* but their operation cannot be understood strictly in their own terms. Rather, we have to look at the social environment in which they operate.

What do we mean by the water quality provision system? First, we include the formal institutional arrangements. Governments — federal, provincial and local — have enacted laws designed to control pollution. To implement these laws, new agencies have been established or old agencies have been assigned new responsibilities. These agencies have adopted procedures for taking specific actions — they have issued regulations governing the activities of those who use this river. Beyond these obvious elements are such things as the structure of taxes and subsidies which encourage investment in pollution abatement. Second, we include the informal and customary relationships that exist for the sharing of responsibilities. That is, where there is a possibility of more than one agency or more than one level of government taking action on a specific issue, there are, typically, informal arrangements for deciding who does what. Third, we include all the activities and their agents, all the interests and their representatives, and all the organized and unorganized groups which have some affect on or concern with the quality of the water in the Lower Fraser River. The River and its basin is a multiple use resource. We use the River, its tributaries and its shores for a variety of purposes: shipping, log transportation and storage, fishing, recreation, the disposal of our wastes, dredging for spoils as a by-product of maintaining navigation channels, industrial water supply, and as sites for industries, harbours and houses. As a result, pollution in the River can be caused by the myriad of activities carried on in the Basin. Some forms of pollution are caused by activities in no way connected with the river: for example, automobiles produce lead which can be washed off roads into the river. Some of the activities, such as commercial and sport fishing, are directly dependent on the continuing health of the river environment.

This large number of uses of the Lower Fraser has led to a wide diversity of interests, which in turn has led to a large number of organizations that are concerned with pollution of the river. We have been able to identify about 40 different government agencies, private organizations and groups that play some role in the way in which water quality is managed. For some, the Fraser is of prime concern, for others it is peripheral, and there is no neat dividing line between resource protection interests and waste disposal interests. Moreover, there is a great deal of diversity among groups whose interests appear superficially to be the same. The fact that this wide range of interests exists in the water quality provision system has far reaching significance for the way the institutional arrangements for the control of pollution can and do function in the Lower Fraser.

Fish boats at Steveston.   Fitch Cady

With this background in mind on the wide diversity of interests concerned with the river, how do we evaluate the performance of institutional arrangements for pollution control? While a substantial number of considerations could enter into such an evaluation we will limit ourselves in this chapter to three:

1. The representation of interests
2. The adequacy of information for decisions
3. Administrative efficiency

Let's expand briefly on what we mean by each of these considerations. The first point, *the representation of interests,* refers to the fact that some of the uses of the river are incompatible with others. Toxic wastes threaten the salmon fishery and log storage interferes with bar fishing, for example. Are there acceptable procedures for resolving these conflicts? How do they work? Is any group or interest excluded for one reason or another? As in other public matters, we maintain that government efforts to control pollution should reflect what society wants. But individual members of society have different preferences as they relate to pollution. Some, no doubt, would like a pristine river; some would like to take full advantage of the economies they would realize through discharging wastes to the river, and most of us fall somewhere in between. We look to our institutions to weigh these different preferences in acceptable ways. In trying to assess whether differing interests have been weighed satisfactorily, we believe that two questions are important. One of these may be expressed as follows:

Do pollution control decisions take into account the views of those affected by them?

This question goes beyond the issue of whether organized interests have the opportunity to express their views and is concerned as well with whether the unorganized public's priorities are considered.

The second question raised in connection with the representation of interests relates to the information on which pollution control decisions are based.

Is the information of a type that both organized interests and the unorganized public can arrive at informed judgements about both individual cases and pollution control policy generally as they relate to the Fraser River?

This second question requires special consideration because it is not self-evident what kind of information we require. Let us, therefore, examine what we mean by adequacy of information.

There are three types of information that are necessary to decide what pollution control policies to pursue. *First,* what damages, if any, is pollution causing? *Second,* how can the flow of wastes to the river be controlled or reduced? *Third,* what would it cost to prevent or reduce pollution through the various ways available?

An important feature of the information that we would like to have is its *comprehensiveness.* We should seek as a goal to understand what *all* of the damages are, what *all* the sources of wastes are and how each might be controlled; and what the costs of controlling *each* source would be. Now, Westwater's efforts to provide some of this information, spelled out in earlier chapters, have made it obvious that we will never know all we would like to know about the river. But where we do not have full information we should at the least try to identify the uncertainties and define the risks we take in using the river in potentially harmful ways.

The final consideration, administrative efficiency, is concerned with the relationship between the resources expended and the results achieved from the present system of pollution control. Chapter 6 examined the costs and effectiveness of various ways of altering the flow of wastes to the river. We here are concerned with another aspect of efficiency. One of the costs of pollution control is the cost of administration: the time and effort expended by the many public and private agencies and groups. It is necessary to ask first, whether there is any misplaced time and effort and thus a wasting of resources, given the number of agencies and jurisdictions, and, secondly, whether such time and effort could usefully be reallocated.

To summarize, then, in this chapter we will confine our appraisal of institutional arrangements to the following three questions. Do pollution control decisions sufficiently account for the views of those affected by them? Are pollution control decisions based on comprehensive information? Do pollution control decisions waste administrative time and effort?

The next section will briefly describe the organization and operation of the major institutional arrangements for pollution control, including the legislative and administrative framework and the application of both law and policy. The following section will present a case study of pollution control to illustrate some of the ways in which the water quality provision system operates. We will appraise, in section four, some of the strengths and weaknesses of the present system in the light of the three criteria discussed above, and suggest ways of changing the institutional structure to make it operate better.

INSTITUTIONAL ARRANGEMENTS FOR POLLUTION CONTROL

In this section we shall review first the major legislative authority and supporting administrative structures that presently exist for pollution control in the Lower Fraser at each of the four levels of government: Federal, Provincial, Regional and Local. Then we shall look at how these powers are applied and enforced.

Lesislative-Administrative Framework

Let us then look first at some of the major laws and agencies at each level of government. First the federal government (Fig. 1). Its prime authority for pollution control in the Lower Fraser rests largely with one section of the Fisheries Act which prohibits the discharge into streams of substances deleterious to fish. This prohibition is backed by fines and penalties where such discharges are

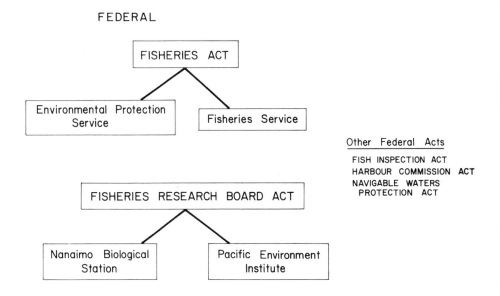

LEGAL FRAMEWORK FOR POLLUTION CONTROL
IN THE LOWER FRASER

FEDERAL

FISHERIES ACT

Environmental Protection Service

Fisheries Service

Other Federal Acts

FISH INSPECTION ACT
HARBOUR COMMISSION ACT
NAVIGABLE WATERS PROTECTION ACT

FISHERIES RESEARCH BOARD ACT

Nanaimo Biological Station

Pacific Environment Institute

Figure 1

proved in a court of law to have taken place. The Fisheries Act also establishes the authority to investigate the possible effects of potential discharges and to recommend design changes to render discharges harmless or, at least, less harmful. In this broader role the Environmental Protection Service with its engineering and waste water treatment expertise and its technology development function play an important part along with the Fisheries Service. Regulations under the Fisheries Act have been drafted for a number of industries in Canada which specify the standards that new plants must meet.

Three other Federal Acts are listed here which have a peripheral role in the Lower Fraser: the Fish Inspection Act, which requires fish to be examined for bacteria and toxic elements, such as heavy metals, to protect public health; the Harbour Commission Act and the Navigable Waters Protection Act which establishes responsibility for harbour maintenance and clean-up, including deliberate and accidental spills from ships and so on.

At the Provincial level the Pollution Control Act is the centrepiece (Fig. 2). It provides for the establishment of an overseeing Board with an administrative support Branch under a Director of Pollution Control. The Act makes it illegal to discharge wastes to land and air or water without a permit from the Director. The Board is empowered to determine what constitutes a polluted condition, to prescribe standards for effluent to be discharged and to strike technical

LEGAL FRAMEWORK FOR POLLUTION CONTROL IN THE LOWER FRASER.

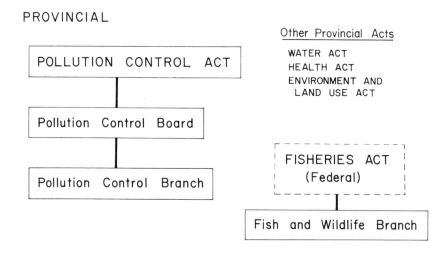

Figure 2

committees necessary to inform itself. The Board issues objectives for industries and municipalities in British Columbia for waste treatment. Administration of the Act is handled by the Pollution Control Branch which receives applications for permits to discharge wastes. It ascertains on technical grounds the likelihood that a potential discharge will meet the requirements established by the Board for that industry. The Branch is also required to forward copies of the application to other provincial government agencies and to take into account their comments or objections.

Other Provincial statutes which have some bearing on pollution control are listed: the Water Act, the Health Act, and the Environment and Land Use Act. This last, especially with the growth of an administrative secretariat, has raised many hopes for resolving water and land use conflicts in British Columbia. In the Lower Fraser, for example, the decision on the type of treatment ultimately to be installed at the Greater Vancouver Sewerage and Drainage District's treatment plant at Annacis Island has been referred to the Environment and Land Use Secretariat. Finally, we need to point out that the provincial Fish and Wildlife Branch's Conservation Officers use the authority of the Federal Fisheries Act.

At the regional and local level, briefly, there exists authority under Municipal sewerage by-laws (Fig. 3). In the Lower Fraser, at least the portion of it within the

LEGAL FRAMEWORK FOR POLLUTION CONTROL IN THE LOWER FRASER

REGIONAL – LOCAL

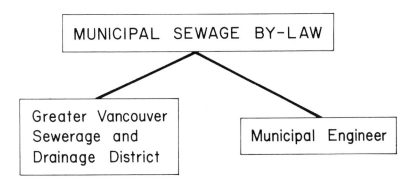

Figure 3

GVRD, the Greater Vancouver Sewerage and Drainage District collects and treats sewage from member municipalities. In order to control what comes in to the treatment plants each municipality enacts a by-law drafted by the Sewerage District and is responsible for ensuring that hook-ups to its sewer meet the by-law standards.

Application and Enforcement

Now that we have the background of the formal legislative authority behind us, we can look more closely at the procedures followed by the agencies: the way they set standards, the way they apply those standards and the way standards are enforced.

At the *Provincial* level the Pollution Control Board establishes objectives for five classes of dischargers (e.g. the food processing industry), which are based on internal technical studies and public hearings at which municipalities, interest groups, and private citizens make presentations as well as companies and trade associations. A panel of experts which attends the hearings is responsible for translating the diverse presentations into a set of objectives. The objectives thus represent a combination of technological, financial, and environmental considerations. Three "schedules" are established. Level C has requirements which every plant in the industry is expected to meet. Level B states what would be desirable to achieve from existing plants within a reasonable length of time and Level A lists the requirements for new plants and the ultimate objectives for existing ones. These objectives are revised every five years on the basis of new information.

Standards are also devised, in loose terms, for receiving waters. The business of mating the two, that is, of trying to ensure that wastes do not degrade the water, is done through the permit process which states what quantity and quality of wastes may be discharged. This process merits some attention since it has become the major administrative device for pollution control in B.C. (see Fig. 4).

When a discharger applies to the Pollution Control Branch for a permit, the first step is typically to hire a consultant to estimate the amount and type of effluent produced by the plant, as required by the application forms. The Pollution Control Act requires the Branch, upon receipt of the application, to forward copies to the Comptroller of Water Rights and the Deputy Ministers of the Department of Health, Agriculture and Recreation and Travel Industry. By convention, the Environmental Protection Service of the Federal Department of the Environment also receives a copy. A copy of the application is published in the B.C. Gazette which is monitored by wildlife and conservation groups.

Each of the agencies initially informed passes the information on to others. The Provincial agencies notify their field offices. The Environmental Protection Service notifies the operations branch of Federal Fisheries, which in turn asks for input from its field officers, Fisheries Research agencies and the International Pacific Salmon Fisheries Commission. If the other agencies do not object, the Pollution Control Branch processes the permit application on the basis of the

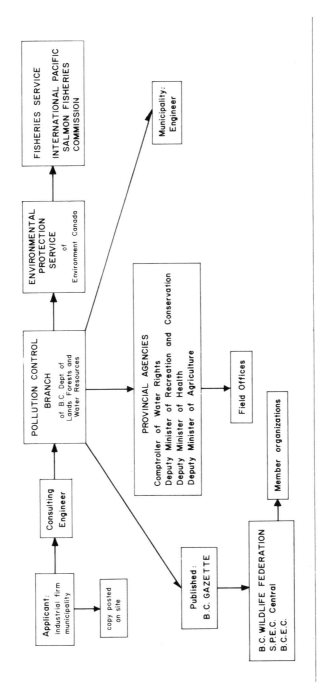

Figure 4 Applications for a permit to discharge wastes circulate through several agencies.

guidelines established by the Board, and what it knows of conditions in the river through its water quality monitoring. When objections are received, the Branch tries to take them into account in the conditions it attaches to permits.

The different interests are accounted for in this process at various stages, depending on the intensity of the conflict. If all the objections can satisfactorily be incorporated into the permit by the Pollution Control Branch, the matter ends there. If they cannot, meetings may be arranged by the Director to try to accommodate them further. Beyond this, appeals to any permit issued by the Director can be made first to the Pollution Control Board, to the Provincial Cabinet, and to the courts. Note that these procedures apply also for *dischargers* who object to the conditions of the permit. Apart from these formal procedures other ways of making oneself heard have evolved. These include obtaining the political support and pressure of elected officials, for example, the mayor and council of the local municipality, taking the case to the media in order to put pressure on provincial politicians and, in the case of government departments, establishing negotiating meetings between deputy ministers and ministers.

An important point to note here is the information which is contained on the permit application. It states what kinds of effluent the applicant intends to discharge and where he intends to discharge it. Alternatives for treatment, or point of discharge are not among the considerations. At present the onus is on the other agencies to estimate what the effects of the discharge will be on the river. Provincial agencies, like the Fish and Wildlife Branch, find it difficult to make more than, in their own words, token comments on the applications referred to them. Needless to say, many groups outside government such as the wildlife and conservation groups are much less able to estimate the importance of proposed discharges. Some Federal agencies are better equipped to respond. However, what is striking about the whole permit process is the narrow, technical issues which it raises.

Once a permit is granted, how is it enforced? It is illegal to discharge wastes not mentioned on the permit or to exceed the amounts specified by the permit. The discharger is required to submit regular samples of its effluent, and the Branch also takes samples, at irregular, unannounced intervals of the same effluent. In general, it is virtually impossible to detect or lay blame for deliberate violations, such as dumping a tank of acid in the river at night. Unintentional violations, for example where the treatment process malfunctions, are, in the opinion of the Pollution Control Branch, dealt with much more effectively by dealing directly with the offending plant rather than through the courts.

At the *Federal* level the same three procedures of standard setting, application and enforcement are followed but somewhat differently. First, in standard setting, the effluent standards apply to the whole of Canada and they are based largely on internal studies of the Environmental Protection Service, with additional information supplied by industry. Because they are Canada-wide they are more general and often weaker than the B.C. guidelines. For the fish processing industry, for example, the Federal standards take into account the economic position of East Coast plants which tends to be weaker than that of B.C. plants.

The standard for receiving waters is established by the Fisheries Act — nothing can be discharged which is deleterious to fish. The Federal effluent standards thus have specific requirements for testing the toxicity to fish of effluent. The B.C. guidelines also state that no toxic elements are to be discharged and provide bioassay standards for each type of discharger.

Because B.C. has it own pollution control permit procedures for implementing standards, Federal standards are applied largely through the B.C. procedures. Where Federal standards are more stringent than the Provincial ones the Environmental Protection Service cooperates with the Pollution Control Branch in seeing that they are incorporated in the permit, including the specific requirements on toxicity.

Information on the effects of discharges on the ecosystem comes primarily from the Federal Fisheries and Marine Service. Results of research work by the Fisheries Research Board, Pacific Environment Institute and International Pacific Salmon Fisheries Commission on the effects of certain effluents on salmon and other fish species are applied by habitat protection biologists in their comments on permit applications. Other branches of the Department of the Environment do in-stream monitoring of water quality which contributes to knowledge about river conditions. However, much of this information is piecemeal. There has been no systematic effort to relate different discharges to effects on the river itself. We can say further that the resources devoted to research on these questions have been very modest. The business of actually commenting on the permit applications as they come along has resulted in staff increases, but nothing like a proportional increase in the knowledge that informs those comments.

Enforcement of the Federal Fisheries Act rests primarily on the shoulders of the field officers. Prosecutions under the Fisheries Act are more numerous than under the Pollution Control Act but the same problems of gathering evidence and identifying responsibility apply. Federal officials, like Provincial ones, prefer, as a general strategy, to work with offenders or potential offenders using the authority of the Act to give them negotiating power.

Let us now look briefly at the *Regional-Local* level. We noted above that the Greater Vancouver Sewerage and Drainage District holds pollution control permits for the sewage treatment plants discharging to the river. Meeting its permit requirements involves first and foremost the proper operation of the plants within the District and this is the main reason behind the sewerage by-law which member municipalities require industries to meet. Certain types of effluent, like metals from an electroplating plant and oils and greases, can kill the bacteria in the digesters of a primary plant, necessitating shutting it down and cleaning it out.

Sewage treatment is the first priority at this level but the control of what goes into the sewers and treatment plants is becoming increasingly important for the control of what finally ends up in the river. Conventional treatment plants are

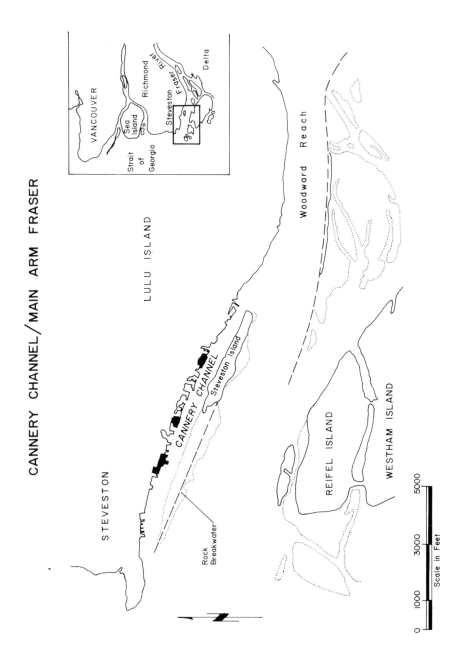

Figure 5

ineffective in removing some toxic wastes. It is Pollution Control Branch policy to get as many direct dischargers as possible to discharge their effluents instead to sewers. The authority of municipalities to control wastes at their source is therefore essential. However, the resources applied by the municipalities to the implementation of their by-laws are extremely modest. The structure of institutional arrangements for pollution control is hence weakest at its most critical stage — that is, disposing of toxic wastes in their least harmful way at the source.

A CASE STUDY: CANNERY CHANNEL

To shed more light on the actual workings of the procedures outlined above we shall look at a particular case, that of Cannery Channel at Steveston where the B.C. Packers Imperial Plant has been trying to meet its obligations under a pollution control permit. Cannery Channel (see Fig. 5) is situated at the mouth of the main arm at Steveston. It is called Cannery Channel because historically there were six or seven fish canneries operating on the channel (north of Steveston Island) although only one major one remains.

Fish processing produces an oily, bloody effluent with varying quantities of remains, such as heads, fins, scales, and guts. The precise effluent quality depends on the recovery and treatment processes appended to the packing plant. Traditionally, the plants were crude and basic, concern for the receiving water

Fraser Main Arm and Cannery Channel looking west.   Fitch Cady

was not prominent and the technology for recovering all but the coarsest wastes to make, for example, fertilizer, was either not available or too expensive compared with the value of the recovered product. The result was aesthetically repugnant during the canning season, but the channel soon returned to a visually natural condition with the natural flushing action of the river. This flushing action probably took care of non-visible water quality problems also, although no test data exist to confirm this conjecture.

When the Pollution Control Act was passed in 1967 few, if any, of the industries which were going to be subject to its terms had a clear idea of what their responsibilities would be. The earlier version of the Act, passed in 1956, applied primarily to municipal waste dischargers in the Lower Fraser. The Iona Sewage Treatment Plant and one at Gilbert Road in Richmond were built to conform to the provisions of the Act. Although the effluent from B.C. Packers is of a type that a municipal sewage plant could treat, the loadings are seasonal in nature and are very large during a short period of time. Richmond Municipality calculated that installing the extra capacity merely for the peak loads from the fish processing plants was not justified. B.C. Packers calculated, in turn, that conventional biological treatment on site would have been very costly, largely because of limited space for the settling ponds. Another alternative, simply piping the waste into the main channel of the river which would easily assimilate them was rejected on the advice of government agencies for fear of interfering with dredging and navigation.

The fish processing industry in general and B.C. Packers in particular approached the Fisheries Research Board to help find alternative means of treating their wastes. An engineer at the Fisheries Research Board began experiments at that time which evolved into a combination of fine screening and physical-chemical treatment of fish processing wastes. Fine screening was intended to take out most of the solids as well as reduce the oxygen consuming BOD loadings to the river; the physical-chemical treatment process would further remove BOD and suspended solids. A full demonstration of these techniques was undertaken at B.C. Packers with the consent of both the Federal Environmental Protection Service and the B.C. Pollution Control Branch. Results of these studies were submitted to the Pollution Control Board's hearings into objectives for the entire food processing industry. Level A requirements under the Pollution Control Board's guidelines were based on the experimental results of 75% removal of BOD and suspended solids.

B.C. Packers were granted a Pollution Control Permit for the discharge of their wastes which called for the installation of fine screening equipment on June 15, 1974 and physical-chemical treatment by June 15, 1975. The coarser wastes at B.C. Packers were already being put into a reduction process to produce fish meal; the addition of fine screening meant that more of this material could be recovered with a reduction of both the BOD loading to the river plus virtually eliminating the slimy deposits on the pilings and on the shore. The application of this technology has been a success.

Salmon Cannery, Steveston ca. 1900.

B.C. Archives

Cannery Channel looking east.

Doug Miller

The application of physical-chemical treatment met with much less success. The consulting engineers hired by B.C. Packers to operate the equipment were unable to achieve the objectives of 75% removal of BOD and suspended solids. During the 1974 season they had difficulty getting better than 30% removal of BOD. On this basis, B.C. Packers applied for a delay in meeting the permit requirements. The Pollution Control Branch at first turned this down and the Environmental Protection Service too recommended that no delay be granted. The plant is still not sure what its position is. During the 1975 season, when it was supposed to be in full compliance with the permit, it again operated the treatment works and got better results, but still not up to the standard set for BOD.

Since the treatment equipment had been tested on site, why couldn't the results have been duplicated by the consultants? One explanation is that the loadings of a fish processing plant are not constant; they change with the type of fish being processed, even with the ripeness of particular catches. Physical-chemical treatment requires fairly sophisticated operation and careful attention given that the waste stream changes in quality. The consultants claim that the experimental results were achieved with stable waste loadings. The engineer who conducted the experiments claimed that the consultants operated the equipment improperly and that buffers attached to the equipment would eliminate the variable loadings of the effluent. It is not necessary to judge the validity of these claims to observe the focus of the argument. It centres on the effectiveness of treatment for reducing loadings. It does not discuss the effects of different levels of discharge on the channel itself. Thirty per cent removal may be enough; 75 per cent removal may be inadequate. The technologically derived objective cannot tell us.

Other than the aesthetic problems apparent in Cannery Channel and the perception of less obvious water quality problems, what in fact was known about the quality of the water? One thing seems certain: little was known before work on treatment processes began. Subsequent monitoring suggested that the B.C. Packers discharge caused some oxygen depletion in the immediate zone of the outfall which could become more serious under certain conditions if flow were significantly reduced through the channel. Monitoring after the installation of fine screening showed an improvement in oxygen levels as well as aesthetic improvements. Oxygen levels were at or near saturation except for the outfall zone, but even there levels were not low enough to be considered dangerous.

Other developments were taking place in the river about this time which illustrate how damages change when uses change, even when waste discharges remain about the same. The Department of Public Works constructed a weir in the main river above the channel to prevent siltation of the Lulu Island sewage treatment plant's diffusers — the point of discharge for its effluent. This reduces the flow through the channel and thus the effluent dilution. The water is virtually stagnant during parts of the tidal cycle and thus would increase the zone of influence of the discharge.

Downstream from B.C. Packers the Small Craft Harbours Branch of Fisheries is planning a marina on Steveston Island to service fishing vessels and pleasure craft. The installation of fine screening equipment at the plant has virtually eliminated visible fish wastes, but blood water is still an aesthetic problem which concerns the marina planners. They would like to see the best possible treatment at B.C. Packers, including the elimination of blood water.

What does this case tell us about pollution control in the Lower Fraser?

First, it demonstrates how a number of interests become involved in a specific situation and how the control agencies function to deal with a pollution control problem.

Second, it illustrates the technical complexity of controlling pollution caused by one of the sources of waste discharge to the river.

Third, it indicates how changes in the uses made of the river not only affect its quality but also determine demands for specific water quality conditions.

Fourth, it indicates that emphasis is placed upon the establishment of effluent discharge standards on the basis of available technologies rather than basing treatment requirements upon water quality needs in the river.

Thus we can see in this single example not only how difficult it is to produce reliable information on which to base pollution control decisions but also how easy it is to be diverted from a focus upon the desired condition of the river to the technologies of control. It illustrates further the diversity of interests affected and the importance of their involvement in the actions that are taken. And finally, it is evident that a process which involves a member of agencies and interests can become time consuming and costly to those who take part.

A PROPOSAL FOR INSTITUTIONAL CHANGE

At the beginning of this chapter we posed three criteria by which to evaluate the way pollution control institutions operate for the Lower Fraser. These may be stated as follows:

1. Are all interests represented in the decision process?
2. Do institutions produce adequate information?
3. Is the time and effort devoted to pollution control activities efficiently allocated?

We will summarize first our answers to each of these questions and then examine several alternative possibilities for strengthening institutional arrangements.

Representation of Interests

On the basis of our findings, the major decision processes do not exclude any of the organized interests. In part this is a consequence of the formal coordinating mechanisms among the governmental agencies. As our preceding description has indicated, procedures exist for involving the interested government agencies and since these agencies tend to look out for the interests of the groups they serve — e.g. the concern of the Fisheries Services with the protection of the interests of the fishing industry — substantial representation of private interests takes place. Hearings on proposed standards provide further access to decision processes by interested parties. As is explained more fully below, effective participation by various interests is handicapped primarily by deficiencies in information about the consequences of potential pollution control policies and actions rather than by a lack of opportunity to be heard.

Adequacy of Information

Since our findings indicate this to be the most critical weakness of existing institutional arrangements, it is necessary to define as precisely as possible what these deficiencies are. This can be done best by comparing the type of information the current system produces with the information required for making informed judgements about how to control pollution of the river.

An adequate information generating system should be designed to provide the following kinds of information.

1. Data on the quantities of pollutants discharged by various kinds of sources.
2. Estimates of the effects of the various pollutants upon human health and on the aquatic ecosystem.
3. Data on the techniques of reducing the discharge of pollutants and the costs thereof.

The existing system is deficient in providing adequate information in each of these categories. First, it does not generate information on pollutant discharges from non-point sources. As our studies have demonstrated non-point discharges are an important source of pollution in the Lower Fraser. Second, it does not secure information on quantities of toxic materials included in discharges from point sources. Third, there is no systematic effort underway to estimate the effects of pollutants discharged to the river upon the aquatic ecosystem. Agencies concerned with the river have the capability to make such studies and from time to time specific investigations are made, but, under the existing system, no agency is motivated to carry-out the kind of comprehensive investigations of the aquatic eco-system necessary to estimate the effects of pollution. Fourth, the analysis of techniques of pollution control and the estimates of costs of control measures are limited largely to end-of-pipe treatment measures. As indicated in Chapter 6, a fully satisfactory system requires that attention be devoted to source control possibilities as well as to various ways of controlling non-point sources. In brief, the existing system does not provide a sufficiently comprehensive set of data to permit either public agencies or private interest groups to make informed decisions on pollution control matters.

The reason for these deficiencies can be found in the design of the current institutional structure, that is, the allocation of responsibilities to government agencies and the laws, regulations and perceptions which guide their activities. None of the agencies has either the responsibility or motivation to see that a comprehensive set of data for pollution control is generated and the combined activities of the various agencies do not produce this result. Let us endeavour to explain why this is the case.

One might expect the Federal Fisheries and Marine Service and the International Pacific Salmon Fisheries Commission to assume responsibility for understanding the effects of pollution upon the aquatic ecosystem of the Lower Fraser. The responsibility of these agencies is for the protection of the salmon and to a lesser degree other commercial fish species. Since the responsibilities of these agencies extend well beyond the Fraser, and since their resources are limited, they have been motivated to focus upon the species with which they are directly responsible instead of upon the aquatic eco-system as a whole. The Provincial Fish and Wildlife Branch has a broad interest in the river but it has a weak research component and since the Fraser is viewed largely as a salmon river — a federal responsibility — it would have little hope of getting funds for such a research endeavour.

The Federal Environmental Protection Service and the B.C. Pollution Control Branch are organized and directed primarily to controlling discharges from point sources. Neither feels a responsibility for understanding the effects of pollutants upon the aquatic ecosystem. The Pollution Control Branch limits its monitoring to water quality analyses. Both direct their efforts toward getting waste dischargers to meet certain effluent standards and neither has a concern for examining in a comprehensive fashion alternative means of reducing the discharge of pollutants and the costs thereof.

Turning to the regional level, the Greater Vancouver Sewerage and Drainage District and its member municipalities are concerned with the collection, pumping and treatment of domestic, commercial and industrial sewage. It is not their responsibility to protect the aquatic environment any more than this is the responsibility of an industrial waste discharger.

From this description two conclusions can be drawn. First, some of the responsibilities for generating the information required for sound pollution control decisions are not clearly assigned to any single agency. No one, for example, feels a responsibility for generating information on non-point sources of pollution. Second, since some of the important responsibilities are shared — particularly the responsibility for understanding the effects of pollutants upon the aquatic ecosystem — no agency feels fully responsible for seeing that an adequate job is done. When it is in the collective interest of a diverse group to produce comprehensive information and yet it is not in the interest of any single member of the group to do it alone, we know from both theory and observable practice that it will be done inadequately or even not done at all.

Efficiency of Administration

There are no obvious instances of waste, duplication of effort, or inefficiencies in the functioning of the agencies concerned with pollution control in the Lower Fraser. The fact that a number of agencies are involved in the control of pollution might lead one to suspect that a substantial amount of overlap in activities takes place. Actually existing procedures for coordination of agency activities appears to prevent any duplication of work performed.

A question does arise as to whether effort is efficiently allocated. It is difficult to answer this question on the basis of information produced by this study. It is significant, however, that a great deal of effort is devoted to the processing and review of effluent discharge permit applications. In view of the limited knowledge of the effects of pollutants on the aquatic ecosystem, one is led to wonder whether it might be more productive to reallocate a portion of the time devoted to the processing of applications to research on the effects of pollutants.

Alternatives for Strengthening Institutional Arrangements

There are a large number of possible ways of strengthening institutional arrangements for control of pollution in the Lower Fraser. There follows a brief examination of several of these and concludes with one which appears to us to be the most promising.

1. *Enlarging the resources available to existing agencies so that more comprehensive information can be provided.*

   Since there is no evident duplication of effort and since the inadequacy of information produced is a major deficiency of the existing system, it is reasonable to ask whether this approach would solve the problem. There is no doubt that an enlargement of the resources available to federal and provincial agencies would be useful. At the same time it is doubtful that this step by itself would be sufficient. First, as previously noted none of these agencies feel a responsibility for dealing with non-point sources or for considering a full range of control technologies. Second, with regard to research on the aquatic environment it is doubtful that these agencies could severally maintain a long range comprehensive effort. One reason is that no recognized centre of leadership exists to see that a comprehensive program is formulated. Another reason is that each agency is periodically confronted with "brush-fire" problems to solve. When an issue of pressing concern to a Federal or Provincial Department comes up, the agency has no alternative but to divert its funds and investigative staff to this issue.

2. *An independent research agency like Westwater.*

   We obviously feel that some of the things Westwater has done and the way it has gone about its studies would be relevant to whatever institutional structure is proposed to fill in the gaps in information about the Lower Fraser. Even if an institute such as Westwater had secure funding — which Westwater does not have — it could not remedy fully the institutional deficiencies that we have identified.

   Of foremost importance, some means must be found to provide a leadership role in seeing that a comprehensive set of information is provided. An independent research centre is unlikely to be motivated to provide such leadership and the other agencies are unlikely to accept the leadership of such an independent body. Beyond this critical deficiency is the additional point that a research group tends to be more oriented toward issues that are of scholarly significance than to those of practical importance. In recognition that its strength lies in advancing knowledge in new areas,

Westwater itself is looking toward a new project which will build upon the work which it has done on the Lower Fraser but not constitute a continuation of that effort.

3. *Implementation of Part II of the Canada Water Act*
The Canada Water Act of 1970 provides for the establishment of regional water pollution control authorities. These agencies can be established through the joint action of the federal and provincial governments or, under some circumstances, through the uni-lateral action of the federal government. If such an agency were established for the Lower Fraser, it would presumably undertake the research and investigative activities required and control the discharge of pollutants to the river. Does this legislation provide a suitable basis for strengthening institutional arrangements in the Lower Fraser? We doubt that it does.

It is noteworthy that this section of the Canada Water Act has never been implemented in any region of the country and we suspect that there are good reasons for this. There is a wide diversity of interests concerned with the control of pollution. One of the virtues of the existing system of federal and provincial agencies is that it provides for the representation of many if not all of these interests in the decisions that are made. While the regional pollution control agency might generate more adequate information, it seems doubtful that it would provide as good a representation of diverse interests as the existing system does.

Closely related to this point are the realities of our federal system. Is any provincial government going to be willing to give up some of its authority to a jointly established federal-provincial entity and would any federal government dare establish such an authority unilaterally? Furthermore, would the fisheries interests — so well represented by the Fisheries and Marine Service and the Environmental Protection Service — be willing to see authority delegated to an independent agency over which they might have much less influence? Thus we see the demand for representation of various interests in decision processes militating against the establishment of a regional pollution control authority for the Lower Fraser.

4. *An independently funded, regionally based, leadership entity*
Our preceding analysis indicates that a new agency will be required to do the job of providing comprehensive information about the Fraser River. It will not replace existing agencies, although it may assume some of the functions of existing agencies, but rather it would become part of the institutional network. How it should be financed and staffed, how it should relate to existing agencies, how it should be controlled, how it should be guided by existing political institutions are all questions which require careful analysis and thought. We offer some ideas for consideration and refinement.

a. *Financing* could be done through one level of government, or a tri-level agreement, but to achieve the necessary degree of independence a fruitful option would be financing through an effluent fee. A modest charge based

Doug Miller

Fisheries and Marine Service. DOE.

on the volume of discharge would produce sizable revenues without burdening individual dischargers. The largest discharger, the GVSDD could pass its charge along to the contributors to its collection system. Not only is an independent source of funding assured, the costs are borne by those who create the uncertainties in the river.

b. *Staffing*. Here we would refer to Westwater as a useful model. An interdisciplinary group under a Director which includes engineering, biological and economic expertise would be in a position of being able to react critically and sensibly to the other agencies and would have internal critical checks on its own programme, by virtue of its interdisciplinary nature, as well as the ability to mount and supervise monitoring and investigative work.

c. *Relationship to Existing Agencies*. The success of a modest enterprise like this will depend on its ability to cooperate with existing agencies on joint data collection and laboratory analysis. We have noted elsewhere the tendency towards such cooperation where interests are shared. Obviously a great deal of care and diplomacy will be needed to ensure that the establishment of such an agency does not produce antagonisms that prejudice the development of inter-agency interaction.

d. *Political Control*. So far we have suggested that the agency should be regionally based, but have said nothing about the level of government to which it should be politically accountable or indeed whether it should have direct political control at all. A politically independent agency, like a crown corporation, has many advantages. It can be set up to pursue a particular objective, given a source of funds and then left alone to do its work. But there are disadvantages too, like the difficulty of altering its course, should that in time appear necessary, for it like any other organization will develop its own goals and motivations.

It is the regional level at which developments which affect the river are felt. Thus there is an argument for making a Fraser River authority subject to the GVRD Board but separate from the GVSDD. This would install some political control over the direction of the agency but keep it separate from one of the major interests on the river, sewage collection and disposal. The concluding chapter in this volume makes some specific suggestions for the organization, funding and responsibilities of such an agency.

SUMMARY AND CONCLUSIONS

We have reviewed the major laws at the Federal, Provincial and Local levels of government, and have described the organization and operation of the administrative agencies that implement these laws for the control of pollution for the Lower Fraser. We have illustrated the major directions and concerns of these institutional arrangements through the case of the B.C. Packers fish processing plant in Richmond. And we have, finally, appraised this system of pollution control in the light of three criteria, and suggested some remedies for the more obvious deficiencies in the system.

But we must conclude with a note of caution. Westwater's biological and chemical studies have continually stressed the uncertainties that exist about the types of pollutants that find their way into the River, and about the effects of these pollutants on the aquatic ecosystem in the short and long run. We must stress that the institutional arrangements that can best provide the system of pollution control that is needed for the conditions of the Lower Fraser are similarly uncertain. Laws, policies and administrative structures may well have to undergo continual reform as the consequences of their operations for the water quality environment are revealed in practice. Such reform is needed now; such reform will in all likelihood be needed in the future. Given the adequacy of our knowledge about the effects of different kinds of institutional arrangements on the environment and its control, we must not expect any ideal system of pollution control to be instituted as a result of our findings. But we can and must expect our elected and administrative officials to adjust continually our institutional arrangements as new evidence about their performance is revealed. Only in this way can we anticipate living in harmony with the Fraser River through its uncertain future.

REFERENCES

Franson, R.T.; Blair, D.; and Bozzer, R. 1976. The Legal Framework for Water Quality Management in the Lower Fraser River of British Columbia. In *Managing the Water Environment,* ed. Neil A. Swainson, pp. 54-95. Vancouver: University of British Columbia Press.

Sproule-Jones, M. and Peterson, K. Institutional and Intergovernmental Arrangements and the Management of Water Quality: The Lower Fraser River Case. Westwater Research Centre, Vancouver, (in preparation).

— —. and — —. 1975. Theoretical Perspectives. Working Paper no. 1. Westwater Research Centre, Vancouver, (draft).

— —. and — —. 1975. Methodology. Working Paper no. 2. Westwater Research Centre, Vancouver, (draft).

FEDERAL STATUTES

1. Canada Water Act R.S.C. 1970 C.52 S1.
2. Fisheries Act and Regulations. R.S.C. 1970 C.F.-14

PROVINCIAL STATUTES

1. Environment and Land Use Act, 1971.
2. Pollution Control Act and Regulations. 1967 S.B.C. 1967 C.34 S.1
3. Water Act R.S.B.C. 1960 C.405

8

Toward a More Certain Future for the Lower Fraser

by The Westwater Staff

This concluding paper offers some specific suggestions for dealing with pollution problems in the Lower Fraser. It will begin by highlighting the nature of the problems we have found and the policy issues we face. These highlights will provide the basis for proposing some long range policy goals for pollution control in the Lower Fraser. Then a set of specific suggestions for progressing toward these goals will be outlined.

HIGHLIGHTS OF THE POLLUTION CONTROL PROBLEMS

The nature of the pollution control problems in the Lower Fraser may be briefly summarized as follows:

First, the most distinguishing feature of these problems is the uncertainty that exists about the consequences for human health and aquatic ecosystems of waste discharges to the river. We know a great deal about the kinds and quantities of pollutants reaching the river. We know that bacterial pollution reaches levels that are considered unsafe to human health and that toxic materials are accumulating in biological organisms. Yet, we know relatively little about many materials suspected of being toxic and no one can say with confidence how serious the effects of the materials being discharged into the river are for both human health and the health of the aquatic ecosystem. It is sobering to realize that in analyses of water, sediments, and the tissues of organisms, evidence is found of numerous substances which cannot be readily identified so that no basis exists for estimating their effects.

Second, the major sources of pollution are associated with urban-industrial development. This applies to most categories of pollutants, including pesticides which one might have expected to be more prevalent in the agricultural areas. It means that the most serious problems in the Lower Fraser stem from activities in the Greater Vancouver region.

Third, toxic wastes pose the greatest long range pollution threat to the ecological system of the Lower Fraser. This observation applies to the Brunette system as well as to the main channels of the river. It is important to keep in mind that substantial quantities of such wastes are in run-off from streets and land areas as well as in effluent from treatment plants. Also, it is noteworthy that the quantities of toxic materials in the effluent of industrial plants which discharge directly into the river system are not known, because adequate information does not appear on the permits or permit applications for such discharges. The conclusion that toxic materials pose a threat to the river's ecological system is substantiated by both the biological studies and the studies of the chemistry of water and sediments conducted by the Centre.

Fourth, bacterial pollution will likely continue to make the Lower Fraser unsuitable for water contact activities, even with the full operation of the treatment plants at all communities along the river. The major sources of bacterial pollution that will remain are (1) runoff from streets and land areas that does not go through treatment plants, (2) the untreated overflow from the Iona treatment plant which by-passes the treatment facilities when storms occur and, (3) sanitary sewers which through error are connected to storm sewers. The Iona plant does not have the capacity to treat the large quantities of effluent which are received during storms, because the sanitary sewers are combined with the storm sewers in the area served by the plant. Thus some raw sewage is discharged directly into the waterway when storms occur.

Fifth, low levels of dissolved oxygen are evident in the slower moving portions of the agricultural tributaries and there are some early signs of eutrophication as the result of excessive nutrients. In some reaches of these tributaries bacterial pollution limits safe recreational use. These forms of pollution are associated with residential developments which use septic tanks and livestock land uses in close association with the streams. It is noteworthy that the most serious pollution found in tributary watersheds has been associated with urban-industrial land uses.

Fitch Cady

Sixth, the effectiveness of pollution control efforts in the Lower Fraser is seriously limited because existing institutional arrangements do not produce a comprehensive attack on pollution problems in the river. A number of agencies have responsibilities relating to the control of pollution in the Lower Fraser and each agency, to our knowledge, is performing its specific functions in a conscientious fashion. However, the current distribution of functions and responsibilities does not provide an overall program which advances steadily our understanding of the effects of pollution upon the river's ecosystem nor does it develop and implement a comprehensive control programme.

POLICY ISSUES

The policy issues we face flow from the characteristics of the pollution problem that have been presented. They revolve around the question of how to reduce the risks to human health and the aquatic ecosystem from existing and prospective levels of pollutant discharges to the river and its tributaries. Broadly speaking we can reduce this risk by two approaches—neither one of which precludes the other. One approach is to increase our knowledge of the effects of pollutants upon human health and aquatic ecosystems and then control pollution to levels found to be safe. The other approach is simply to reduce greatly the discharge of wastes suspected of having damaging effects. It appears only prudent to pursue both of these approaches. If we are to manage water quality in the Lower Fraser wisely, we should develop a good understanding of the effects of pollutants upon the aquatic ecosystem. Yet, even if we mount a major programme of ecological research, many years of effort will be required to unravel the complexities of the river's ecosystem and it is most unlikely that perfect knowledge of the system will ever be achieved. It is only logical, therefore, that we should engage in a programme of investigation and research that will aid us in managing water quality more wisely while at the same time proceeding on the basis of information now available to reduce pollutant discharges to levels that minimize the risk to human health and aquatic ecosystems.

This postulation of the policy problem is the basis for suggesting three broad policy issues with which we must seek to deal. These can be expressed as follows:

1.   *What kind of programme should be undertaken to control pollutant discharges to the river system so as to minimize the risk to human health and to the aquatic ecosystem?*

2.   *What kind of programme of ecological research should be undertaken to aid us in conducting human activities so that they will be in harmony with a healthy aquatic ecosystem?*

3.   *What kind of institutional arrangements do we require to conduct these two programmes effectively and efficiently?*

LONG RANGE GOALS AND A STRATEGY OF ACTION

These three policy questions cannot be answered in a simple straightforward manner because they have many ramifications.

This leads us to suggest that the Province and the people who live in the Lower Fraser Valley should establish some long range goals and adopt a strategy for achieving them. The nature of the problem we face may be likened to the challenges that confronted the early explorers. Here it is appropriate to use Simon Fraser and his exploration of the Fraser River to illustrate our point.

You will recall that his objective—his long range goal—was to reach the mouth of the Columbia. He did not know the way there, he did not know what difficulties he might encounter in trying to reach it, and as we know he reached the mouth of the Fraser instead of the mouth of the Columbia. The important point to us is that he had a long range target, and a strategy of exploration which he followed to pursue his goal. While he did not reach his original goal, it motivated him to accomplish one of the greatest feats in the history of exploration on this continent.

What long range goals and what kind of strategy should we adopt for dealing with the policy questions we face in the Lower Fraser? Our proposed goals are these:

1. *To eliminate from municipal and industrial effluents and land run-off all materials which in light of current knowledge are considered to be toxic to aquatic organisms.*
2. *To enhance water quality in the Lower Fraser and its tributaries so that water contact activities, such as the handling of fishing equipment and bathing, can be engaged in without risk to health.*
3. *To advance our knowledge of the aquatic ecosystem of the Lower Fraser and its tributaries so that within a decade a much better basis will exist for estimating the effects of pollutants upon the aquatic ecosystem.*

You may find these long range goals unacceptable, but it is urged that, even if these goals are not viewed as the correct ones, some general goals should be adopted to motivate and guide the activities that the enhancement of water quality in the Lower Fraser will require. We will, however, use these three goals as the basis for the specific suggestions we will offer. Before proceeding to outline these suggestions, we need to consider the strategy to be pursued in our effort to achieve whatever goals we adopt.

The strategy to pursue, as is the case with most social goals, involves two important components, namely *exploration* and *readjustment*. Since we are unable to determine today what specific measures will best contribute to the realization of our goals, alternative courses of action must be explored. Furthermore, each action considered must be assessed in terms of whether the contribution it will make is worth the cost to be incurred. We should not forget that Simon Fraser did not canoe through the Fraser Canyon after he had estimated the costs that Hells Gate might impose upon him. The programme we undertake — in fact the long range goals we pursue — should be subject to readjustment in light of new knowledge. Our exploratory activities may indicate that existing programmes should be replaced by new ones; research elsewhere may develop new and more effective control measures; our ecological investigations may reveal that substances once thought to be benign are in fact toxic. Thus the strategy we envisage entails a continuous searching for the best way of achieving the goals we seek and the flexibility to alter our course in light of the knowledge we gain.

SPECIFIC PROPOSALS

In outlining some specific suggestions for moving toward the long range goals we have proposed, we are aware of the many things that have already been done or which are being done by public agencies and municipalities and which contribute to the realization of these goals. It is, for example, no small achievement that all municipalities along the Lower Fraser are or soon will be treating their sewage. The monitoring and research that a number of agencies have undertaken contribute significantly to our knowledge of the system with which we are concerned. Our suggestions are made in light of the important work which is already being done. Our proposals will be divided into five categories namely,

— Immediate actions

— Specific further investigations
— Strengthening the tools of management
— Advancing knowledge of the aquatic ecosystem
— Institutional change

Immediate Actions

In addition to the pollution control activities already under way, there are two specific actions that we propose be undertaken immediately to reduce pollution of the Lower Fraser and its tributaries. These are:

1. *The Greater Vancouver Sewerage and Drainage District should initiate a programme to control toxic wastes at their source and prevent their discharge into sewers or to land areas where they might have damaging effects.*

A great virtue of controlling toxic materials at their source is that they are not only kept out of the river but they are also kept out of the sludge. This simplifies the disposal of sludge because if it does not contain toxic materials it can be placed on land without fear that toxic substances may leach into the waterway. Another advantage of source control is the prospect that it is likely to be much less costly than advanced treatment of sewage.

The nature of such a programme and its importance are described in Chapter 6. In brief, it would entail the assignment of a small professional staff to work with commercial and industrial establishments to devise ways and means of keeping toxic wastes out of sewers.

Our studies indicate that the programme could well begin with the metal finishing industry. Once steps have been taken to reduce its toxic discharges, the staff should proceed to work with other industries in order of the significance of their toxic wastes. An important responsibility of such a staff should be to identify those toxic materials which can and should be controlled at the point of manufacture or distribution. This would enable the Greater Vancouver Regional District to request the federal government to take action in accord with the provisions of the recently enacted environmental contaminants legislation.

2. *Existing regulations for the prevention of stream pollution by septic tanks and by drainage from barnyards, feed lots, poultry facilities, stock watering, etc. should be implemented more effectively.*

A highly permeable soil may assure that a septic tank will function effectively in accepting waste volumes but, as our studies strongly suggest, seepage from the drain field may increase nutrient loadings to streams. Thus care must be exercised to locate housing and design facilities so that such loading is unlikely to occur. More effective control of pollution resulting from farming practices is a necessary step to the reduction of bacteria, BOD loadings and nutrient pollution, particularly in the tributary basins. Currently such regulation is the responsibility of agricultural producer associations, but it appears that they act primarily in response to complaints. Our observations indicate that the less noticeable violations are not dealt with through this process.

Fisheries and Marine Services D.O.E.

Specific Further Investigations

Beyond the foregoing immediate actions there are a number of investigations which should be launched to determine the practicability and feasibility of making further reductions in the discharge of polluting materials to the river. These are as follows:

1. *Studies should be launched to determine what kind of additional treatment — beyond primary treatment and the source control programme — is warranted to deal with toxic contaminants in sewage produced in the Greater Vancouver region.*

There are three major issues that these studies need to address: One is whether treatment measures are required to deal with compounds — such as ammonia — known to be acutely toxic to fish under some conditions. While such compounds are found in the effluent of a primary treatment plant it is not clear whether they would have any damaging effects in view of the amount of dilution provided by the Fraser and the fact that they degrade rapidly. A second issue is whether treatment in addition to the primary treatment already provided is warranted to reduce toxic waste discharges to the river beyond the reductions to be achieved through a source control programme. Primary treatment removes some of these toxic compounds and the source control programme should remove still more. Should we seek still further removal through additional stages of treatment? The third issue is concerned with the technology that should be utilized if additional treatment is found desirable. The conventional secondary treatment through biological activated sludge processes entails a large capital investment compared with some chemical processes and reports indicate that chemical treatment may remove a higher percentage of the toxic materials. Since experience with designing treatment facilities to remove toxic materials is limited, pilot studies should be undertaken to determine the relative effectiveness of chemical processes and activated sludge processes before deciding upon the technology to apply.

2. *A study should be made of the desirability of establishing a regional facility for separate collection and disposal of toxic wastes.*

One reason that toxic materials are discharged to sewers is that many plants have no economical disposal alternative. As was pointed out in Chapter 6, some cities in the United States are establishing regional facilities which collect toxic wastes, reclaim materials to the extent feasible, and assure safe disposal of the remainder. Such a facility could constitute an integral part of an effective programme for controlling toxic pollutants at their source. The investigation of this possibility in association with the source control effort merits high priority.

3. *An investigation should be made of alternative means of controlling pollution from urban run-off in the Greater Vancouver region.*

As the Centre's studies have so clearly demonstrated, urban run-off is an important source of both bacterial and toxic pollutants. It is essential, therefore, that alternative possibilities for controlling this source of pollution be carefully examined. Conceivably some major pollutants — such as PCB's — can best be controlled at the point of production and distribution. Possibly land use practices can be regulated to reduce pollution in some areas and the sweeping of streets might be worthwhile in others. Treatment of storm run-off in a region with as much rainfall as Vancouver receives would be costly indeed.

A special problem is faced at the Iona sewage treatment plant because of the necessity to by-pass the plant when its hydraulic capacity is exceeded by the run-off from a storm. This results in untreated sewage being discharged into the mouth of the North Arm. There is not a simple solution to this problem. Conceivably some of the excess flow could be stored in lagoons and treated after the flows have diminished. Seattle has developed procedures for storing some of the excess flows in the sewers themselves through a computerized management system of sewer flow control. A very careful and sophisticated investigation, including cost effectiveness studies of alternative possibilities, should be undertaken and considered before deciding upon the course to pursue.

4. *Studies should be made of additional agricultural tributary basins to ascertain whether problems differ from those found in the Salmon, and if they do, to develop appropriate control measures.*

Studies of the tributary basins were limited to the collection and analyses of water quality data by the Inland Waters Directorate and more detailed studies of the Brunette and Salmon by the Westwater staff. It is quite possible that conditions in the other tributary agricultural basins differ from those found in the Salmon. For example, because of differing physical land conditions and differing agricultural practices, pollution by nutrients and pesticides could be more serious in other basins than they have been found to be in the Salmon. These possibilities should first be checked by undertaking some additional reconnaissance study of each of the agricultural tributaries, and then, if new problems are discovered, more detailed studies of these problems should be made.

Strengthening the Tools of Management

To make sure that desirable water quality conditions are maintained, those responsible for water quality management require certain basic information, and waste producers must be motivated to limit their discharges of polluting materials. We offer the following suggestions for strengthening the instruments for controlling pollution in the Lower Fraser:

1. *The procedures for granting permits to plants to discharge wastes directly to the river should be modified so as to provide an improved foundation for deciding upon the conditions governing each permit. This can be accomplished by:*

    a. *Requiring the waste discharger to provide estimates of the quantities and concentrations of pollutants that would be discharged.*

    b. *Requiring the waste discharger to provide a materials balance account which indicates where all toxic materials end up.*

    c. *Having the Pollution Control Branch furnish the foregoing information to other concerned agencies for review together with its assessment of the environmental impact of the proposed discharge.*

Currently applications for permits do not provide adequate information on the toxic materials used in production processes. The information that the waste discharger would supply would provide the basis for an environmental impact assessment by the Pollution Control Branch, which in turn would aid agency reviewers in their evaluation of permit applications. Steps should be initiated to collect the same information from existing permitees.

2. *A system of economic incentives should be developed which motivates waste producers to limit their discharge of toxic materials to the river. The system should include a special charge that is automatically imposed for discharges of toxic materials in excess of permitted amounts.*

There is a substantial body of literature, to which Westwater has contributed, on the development of economic incentive systems. The proposed system should be so designed that there is a significant economic incentive to each waste producer to reduce the quantities of toxic materials discharged to the river. The incentive should apply to public agencies (including municipal treatment facilities) as well as to private firms. Westwater will be presenting in one of its technical reports an analysis of alternative systems that might be applied in the Lower Fraser.

3. *Dischargers of non-domestic wastes to the sewerage system should be liable to secure a permit and supply information on:*
   a. *Quantities and concentrations of pollutants discharged.*
   b. *A materials balance account which indicates where all toxic materials end up.*

This procedure should be instituted in association with the source control programme and the sewer surcharge system referred to below. As the source control programme proceeds it should be possible to establish the specific classes of waste dischargers in terms of the type of commercial or industrial establishment and size of operation to which these provisions should apply.

4. *A sewer surcharge system should be developed within the Greater Vancouver Sewerage and Drainage District which would:*
   a. *Provide an incentive to reduce the discharge of toxic materials to sewers.*
   b. *Provide an incentive to limit the volume of loadings upon treatment plants.*
   c. *Apportion an appropriate share of the long-run cost of using sewerage facilities and the source control programme to the discharger.*

There is a widespread assumption that if a waste producer discharges to a sewer, the waste disposal problem is automatically handled efficiently and effectively. It is important that a potential discharger to sewers should have an incentive to reduce toxic discharges and that he should take into account the full cost of using the municipal sewerage system. Otherwise he will not be motivated to use the sewerage system efficiently. The sewer surcharge system which has been successfully used elsewhere would provide such an incentive. The administration of the system can be based upon discharge data collected from the permits proposed above.

Advancing Knowledge of the Aquatic Ecosystem

The suggestions that have been made so far have been concerned with reducing and controlling discharges to the river system. However, one of the three long range goals we have proposed is to advance our knowledge of the aquatic ecosystem so that the effects of waste discharges can be estimated with reasonable accuracy. We propose, therefore that:

A continuing programme of ecological investigations of the Lower Fraser should be launched to deepen our understanding progressively over time of this complex and invaluable resource.

This programme is urgently needed, not only because of the threat of pollution to the health of the aquatic environment, but also because of the encroachments of other kinds of development in the Fraser River estuary. Our aim should be to advance our knowledge of this system so that human activities on the Lower Fraser are compatible with a healthy aquatic ecosystem. Such

Brian Gates

knowledge is of fundamental importance to any environmental impact assessment of waste discharges. The programme should take into account the results of research in other parts of the world as well as embracing specific studies of the Lower Fraser.

The management activities outlined above will produce important data on discharges to the river. In addition it is assumed that the Federal Inland Waters Directorate and the B.C. Water Resources Service will continue to monitor at key locations, and a number of agencies, such as the International Pacific Salmon Fisheries Commission, the Federal Environmental Protection Service, and the Federal Fisheries and Marine Service will continue to conduct specific studies. These studies should be taken into account and a programme of additional investigations launched that would produce comprehensive coverage of the system. Westwater's research points up two categories of studies which should be included in this programme. One is a set of physical and biological investigations of sloughs and side channels of the river. It is evident that some of these are important feeding areas for the juvenile salmon, yet little is known about these areas. We also propose that at approximately four to six year intervals, water and sediment analyses and biological studies of the nature conducted by Westwater be repeated at the locations used by the Centre in its studies.

Institutional Change

The most difficult task we face in preserving and enhancing water quality in the Lower Fraser is that of equipping our public agencies with the necessary responsibilities, authorities, capabilities, and motivations to carry out the measures we have proposed in the preceding sections of this presentation. You will recall in Chapter 7 it was concluded that the current distribution of functions and responsibilities among public agencies is such that a comprehensive programme of pollution control simply does not get planned and undertaken. Our basic objective must be to remedy this situation if we are to have any hope for achieving the long range goals we have outlined. We have concluded that in the Lower Fraser the best way to bring this about is through strengthening the capability of the regional districts to complement the work of other agencies, so that pollution control is dealt with on a comprehensive basis. As our studies have revealed, the problems in the tributaries and upstream of the Greater Vancouver region are separate from those within the Greater Vancouver region, where they are more serious and more complex. We will, therefore, suggest a more elaborate institutional mechanism for the GVRD than for the other two regional districts.

A. *The Greater Vancouver Regional District*

In this region it is proposed that:

1. *An Environmental Protection Committee of the Board of the GVRD should be established and that it have a secretariat to carry out the following responsibilities under its direction:*

    a. *To take the lead in developing and conducting a programme of ecological studies designed to provide a deeper understanding of the aquatic ecosystem of the Lower Fraser.*

    b. *To work with federal, provincial and local agencies and other groups in developing a comprehensive programme for preserving and enhancing water quality in the Lower Fraser.*

    c. *To undertake such investigations and studies as are necessary to complement the activities of other agencies so as to assure that a comprehensive programme is in fact undertaken.*

    d. *To make more effective the involvement of the concerned general public and non-professional groups in the pollution control system by:*

        i) *Consultation on the design of the comprehensive programme.*

        ii) *Reporting annually on the progress of the programme.*

        iii) *Providing biennial evaluations of water quality conditions in the river, including an assessment of the causes of any changes from one reporting period to the next.*

        iv) *Assuring that all reports dealing with pollution control in the Lower Fraser are public and have explanatory summaries in lay language.*

2. *Financial support for the Committee and its secretariat should be provided by revenues from a simple charge on effluent discharged directly to the Lower Fraser.*

These proposals have so many implications that they require further elaboration in order to be fully understood.

First, we envisage the secretariat staff as being relatively small — in the range of seven to twelve professional employees.

Second, we propose that this staff be composed of individuals from several disciplines, including engineering, biology, chemistry and economics. At least two well qualified people (including a biologist and an environmental chemist) would be responsible for the continuing ecological studies.

Third, we assume that some of the studies which the committee will wish to undertake should be handled under contract with consulting firms or academic institutions in order to secure the expertise required.

Fourth, it is proposed that the committee support a competitive masters and Ph.D. fellowship programme for students engaged in research relating to pollution control in the Lower Fraser. Such a programme would not only aid in the education of professionals in the area of environmental quality control, but it would help maintain continuing university involvement in research on the Lower Fraser at a very modest cost.

A programme of the nature we have characterized would require a budget something like this:

		Low Estimate	High Estimate
(a)	Support of Committee meetings and activities of Committee members	3,000	5,000
(b)	Staff salaries	210,000	400,000
(c)	Contractual services	100,000	200,000
(d)	Fellowship programme	20,000	40,000
(e)	Space, supplies, equipment, and miscellaneous services	25,000	50,000
		358,000	695,000

We believe that the programme should begin with a secretariat of modest size (such as suggested by the low estimate) with a carefully chosen staff of well qualified people. Then as the programme takes shape consideration could be given to the possible need for expanding it.

Our proposals contemplate the development of special revenues to support the functions of the Environmental Protection Committee. The rationale for this is that under conditions of fiscal stringency, the Committee is unlikely to receive sufficient funding from the general funds available to the District to carry out its responsibilities.

The levying of a simple charge against effluent that goes into the river is fair inasmuch as it is these waste discharges which create the uncertainties that make the committee's functions necessary. At the outset we propose that the charges be based upon the volume of discharge. On the basis of available data, such a charge system designed to produce sufficient revenues to finance the low budget estimate would result in an annual charge of about one half a cent per thousand gallons discharged. For a waste producer discharging about 100,000 gallons of effluent per day the total annual charge would be $182.50. If funds were required to support the high budget estimate the annual charge to each waste producer would be about one cent per thousand gallons discharged.

Once the secretariat is established and steps are being taken to devise the proposed economic incentive system, it may prove practicable to secure the revenues required to support the Secretariat activities from an effluent charge system that would serve both purposes. Still another matter that merits consideration is the possibility of using this same revenue source to help support the pollution control activities of the B.C. Water Resources Service within the District. These matters will be more fully explored in the technical reports to be published by the Centre.

Before leaving the Greater Vancouver Regional District one final point needs to be made. If an Environmental Protection Committee is established, it would only be logical to extend its responsibilities to other waters in the regional district besides those of the Lower Fraser and to other aspects of environmental quality—such as air pollution, noise, and habitat destruction. If these steps were taken it would be important to keep the work of the Committee secretariat quite separate from the operating activities of the Greater Vancouver Regional District in the fields of sewage collection and treatment, air pollution control and solid waste disposal. Experience has demonstrated that the mixing of operating programmes with planning and investigation activities do not work well. We have not studied these possible additions to the committee's responsibilities but we recognize that they merit examination.

B. *Other Regional Districts*

Our studies have indicated that the problems in the agricultural tributaries are not as serious as the problems found in the Greater Vancouver Regional District. Yet, these areas require institutional attention as well. It is with this in mind that the following specific proposal is offered:

Other regional districts in the Lower Fraser area should have an environmental protection officer responsible to the District Board who would:

  a. *Work with other public agencies in developing a comprehensive programme of pollution control.*
  b. *Be assigned responsibility for securing compliance with land use regulations designed to prevent pollution.*
  c. *Review development proposals and waste discharge permit applications and assess their impact on water quality.*

This proposal recognizes the need for a positive programme to control pollution upstream of the Greater Vancouver region in both the main river and the tributaries.

It is envisaged that an environmental protection officer employed by the regional district, instead of the agricultural producer associations, would be assigned responsibility for securing compliance with land use regulations designed to prevent pollution. Furthermore, he should be offered an opportunity to review all developmental proposals and all applications for waste discharge permits so that he can indicate whether approval of such actions would threaten water quality in the region.

SUMMARY AND CONCLUSIONS

In concluding this study of pollution control in the Lower Fraser, we would like to characterize the nature of the choice we face. The river is still in remarkably good shape, in spite of the insults we have given it. We have the time and the capability to eliminate the pollution which makes the river a hazard to health and which threatens to destroy the populations of fish and waterfowl that use this waterway. We can choose between two alternative courses; one would be to proceed much as we have in the past, the other would be to adopt an integrated programme to preserve the aquatic environment of the Lower Fraser. Let us project each of these alternatives as scenarios of the future of the Lower Fraser.

The scenario based upon a continuation of past practice would entail the application of the fire fighting that has typified much environmental management and protection work. One can envisage the urban and industrial development as now found on much of the North Arm spreading over the remaining marsh areas of the Main Arm and up the mainstem of the river. Treatment plants, no doubt, would be enlarged and more advance treatment measures applied. But the likelihood is that the progress of development would introduce an ever increasing and insidious array of chemical by-products which would find their way into the river and these would be too much for the fish and the waterfowl. To be sure there would still be some young salmon rushing downstream to the lower toxicity of the sea and a few adult salmon would still struggle upstream in search of a suitable site amid the "developed" tributaries to spawn. But these would be in the nature of biological curiosities, for the rich productivity of the Lower Fraser would be gone. One can envisage further studies of the nature of the one we have just completed showing the dangers of increasing pollution and these would be read by a few and carefully filed in our libraries.

This scenario is not unlike what has in fact happened in the United States — on the Illinois River, for example. There, surveys were conducted every twenty years or so beginning in the late 19th century but these seem to have done little more than provide a rigorous documentation of river degradation. One can hardly think of a more bitter experience than to have our research serve a similar function for the Lower Fraser.

The alternate scenario is one of hope and promise. It envisages the prevention of encroachment on the marshlands and other special regions of the river required to preserve its ecological systems. It would entail a comprehensive programme for controlling pollution from all sources which would minimize the hazard to the aquatic ecosystem. This type of programme will require investments in control measures, investments in further investigation, and some modest changes in our institutions. But such actions would promise preservation of the salmon runs and other fish and wildlife that the Lower Fraser sustains. It would mean the preservation of a grand river, which together with the mountains and the sea, sets Vancouver above other cities of the world.

We appreciate our own fallibility in dealing with the complex matters we have been studying. There may be errors in some of our analyses, and the suggestions we have made no doubt, can be strengthened in many ways. Yet, because of the value we attach to preserving the water quality of the Lower Fraser, we have full confidence in the principles which underly our specific proposals. They are these:

— We should aim high in establishing our goals for the Lower Fraser.
— We should not run risks with the ecological system of the Lower Fraser in our use and disposal of toxic materials.
— Since we are dealing with a continuously changing, complex system, it behooves us to deepen progressively over time our understanding of this system so as to improve the foundation for decisions designed to preserve and enhance water quality.

— Governmental institutions should be organized and motivated to examine all facets of the pollution problem and to design and implement programmes in light of their relative need and effectiveness.
— Waste producers should be made conscious of the effects of their discharges and should have positive incentives to reduce the damages that their discharges cause.

We believe that if these basic principles are adhered to the future of the Lower Fraser will not be so uncertain.

Beginning of the new. New Westminster ca. 1863.   B.C. Archives

AUTHORS ACKNOWLEDGEMENTS

Acknowledgements by Anthony H.J. Dorcey

The analyses made by Graeme Bethell, during a short-term appointment with Westwater, and by Rosemary Basham, Kathy Friesen and Gary Robinson, whilst employed on Provincial summer student funds, have been invaluable in writing chapter 6. Graeme Bethell reviewed the literature to assess the effectiveness of different municipal treatment plant processes in removing toxic materials. Gary Robinson developed initial estimates of the costs of building and operating these plants including sludge disposal for the GVSDD plants discharging into the Lower Fraser. Kathy Friesen developed estimates of the volume of runoff from areas of the GVRD draining into the Fraser. Rosemary Basham estimated the magnitudes of subsidies available to municipalities and industries under provincial and federal legislation.

Brian Talbot of the Greater Vancouver Sewerage and Drainage District provided information about the District's plants and valuable criticism of the cost-effectiveness analyses.

I am indeed most grateful to Lillian Mack and Fitch Cady for the long hours and great fun that they put into producing a book from a series of lecture texts.

Acknowledgements by Kenneth J. Hall

Many scientists and technicians from the University of British Columbia, federal, provincial and municipal government agencies contributed their time and expertise during the physical-chemical studies conducted by Westwater.

I would like to acknowledge the Water Quality Branch of the Environmental Management Service under the direction of C.H. McBratney for its cooperation in the water quality studies. Special thanks are extended to Fred Mah for supervision of laboratory analysis, Jim Taylor for coordination of sampling and Jim McKinley for expertise in chlorinated hydrocarbon analysis.

Staff of the Civil Engineering Department at UBC participated in various studies on the Fraser. I am indebted to Liza MacDonald of the Pollution Control Laboratory for her advice and cooperation during the water quality studies. Peter Ward, Chris Joy, and Michael Quick supervised and conducted the dye tracer and physical modelling studies. The staff of the civil engineering workshop were very helpful in constructing and repairing field equipment.

The assistance of K. Fletcher of the Geological Science Centre at UBC in providing analytical facilities for trace metal analysis is greatly appreciated.

I am very grateful to Malcolm Clark and William Hamilton of the Pollution Control Branch for providing water and wastewater quality data from their files.

Stan Vernon and the staff of the Greater Vancouver Regional District were very helpful in providing information on various sewerage systems and co-operating during the wastewater sampling programme.

Several students were employed on the Provincial governments summer work programme. These included—John Chan who conducted pesticide analysis on sediments. Kathy Hayward who determined organic compounds in wastewaters and Douglas McLeod who helped to collect and collate data on wastewater sources.

Finally, I want to thank Itsuo Yesaki and Fred Koch at Westwater who were deeply involved with sample collection, analysis and data compilation during all stages of the physical-chemical studies.

Acknowledgements by Thomas G. Northcote

The biological studies summarized in chapter 5 could never have been conducted without the assistance of Kanji Tsumura, Jim Irvine, Tom Johnston and others who spent many hours on the river collecting samples and even longer in the laboratory sorting and analysing them. Tom Johnston also provided much help in computer programming and data preparation. Gordon Ennis and Bill Dunford took an active part in some phases of the work.

Analysis of fish tissues for heavy metals was arranged through Dr. K. Fletcher, Geological Sciences, University of British Columbia, and for chlorinated hydrocarbons through Dr. L. Albright, Biological Sciences, Simon Fraser University. Work on marine invertebrates at the river mouth was undertaken by Carol Bawden, Bill Heath and Angela Norton and was directed by Dr. T. Parsons, Institute of Oceanography, University of British Columbia, Professor J.G. Pendergrast, Biological Sciences, University of Waikato, New Zealand kindly provided facilities for manuscript preparation.

Acknowledgements by Mark H. Sproule-Jones and Kenneth G. Peterson

We would like to thank all the people in government and industry as well as private individuals who gave freely of their time in the course of our investigations. We interviewed over 100 people and obviously cannot list them here but their cooperation made our work possible. We would also like to thank members of the Westwater staff who made helpful suggestions throughout the study and who helped us through technical aspects quite beyond our expertise. Four research assistants, Tom Ferguson, Bonnie Cowan, Bob Coulter and Russ Freethy also deserve mention for their work on the citizen survey.

Acknowledgements by John H. Wiens

The author wishes to acknowledge with sincere appreciation the work of Ms. Roxanna Beale, Dr. L.M. Lavkulich, Dr. H.O. Slaymaker and Dr. K.J. Hall which formed the basis for some of the methodology and results presented in my part of chapter 4. Analytical water chemistry results are largely those of Ms. Beale whereas the land use and geomorphic unit mapping referred to was directed by Drs. Lavkulich and Slaymaker. Dr. Hall kindly provided information on chlorinated hydrocarbon analysis.

BIOGRAPHICAL NOTES

Anthony H.J. Dorcey is an Assistant Director of the Westwater Research Centre. After obtaining an MA in Economics from the University of Aberdeen, Scotland, he went to the University of Wisconsin where he obtained an MS in Regional Planning and worked on an interdisciplinary project on water quality management in the Wisconsin River Basin. He has published a variety of articles on the design and implementation of water quality management policies.

Irving K. Fox is Director of the Westwater Research Centre and Professor in the School of Community and Regional Planning at UBC. Since completing graduate work in political science at the University of Michigan, he has worked and written on problems of water resources management throughout North and South America, in Europe and the Soviet Union. For five years he led river basin studies of the U.S. Department of the Interior and for seven years he was Vice-President of Resources for the Future, Inc. Afterwards at the University of Wisconsin, while Associate Director of the Water Resources Center and Chairman of the Department of Urban and Regional Planning, he directed an interdisciplinary study of water quality management in the Wisconsin River Basin. In 1971 he came to UBC to develop the Westwater Research Centre and launch its first major interdisciplinary project, the results of which are reported in this book. In 1975 he was appointed to the Canadian Environmental Advisory Council.

Kenneth J. Hall is an Assistant Director of the Westwater Research Centre and an Assistant Professor in the Department of Civil Engineering at UBC. After obtaining a BSA from Ontario Agricultural College he obtained a doctorate in Water Chemistry from the University of Wisconsin. He came to UBC as a post-doctoral fellow in the Institute of Animal Resource Ecology and worked on the Marion Lake IBP project. He has published a variety of articles on the chemistry of natural materials and pollutants in aquatic environments.

Thomas G. Northcote is a Professor at UBC with appointments in the Faculty of Forestry, Institute of Animal Resource Ecology and the Westwater Research Centre. He was born and raised in the Lower Fraser Valley and obtained his doctorate in Zoology from UBC. Before coming to the university full-time he was in charge of the Research Division of B.C. Fish and Wildlife Branch. He is the author of more than forty publications on the biology of fisheries in British Columbia.

Kenneth G. Peterson is a Research Associate with the Westwater Research Centre. After obtaining a BA in Economics from UBC and an MA from Northwestern University, he worked as a Research Economist firstly with Pearse Bowden Economic Consultants and then with the Fisheries Service, Environment

Canada. He has written several reports on the evaluation of pollution control and recreation policy.

Mark H. Sproule-Jones is an Associate Professor in the Political Science Department at the University of Victoria. After obtaining a B.Sc. from the London School of Economics and Political Science, he obtained his doctorate in Political Science from Indiana University. During a sabbatical in '74-'75 he was a Visiting Research Associate with the Westwater Research Centre. He is the author of a variety of publications on urban politics and public policy evaluation.

John H. Wiens is Assistant Professor in the Soil Science Department at UBC. He was born and raised in the Lower Fraser Valley. After obtaining a BSA and MSc in Soil Science from UBC he studied for a doctorate in Soil Science at Oregon State University.

WESTWATER PUBLICATIONS

BOOKS

Swainson, N.A., ed. 1976. *Managing the Water Environment.* Vancouver: U.B.C. Press.

LeMarquand, D. *Politics and Planning of International Rivers.* (Forthcoming, 1976).

Stephenson, J.B., *The Practical Application of Economic Incentives to the Control of Pollution: The Case of British Columbia.* Vancouver: U.B.C. Press. (In press).

TECHNICAL REPORTS

Bawden, C.A.; Heath, W.A.; and Norton, A.B. *A Preliminary Baseline Study of Roberts and Sturgeon Banks.* Technical Report No. 1.

Benedict, A.H.; Hall, K.J.; and Koch, F.A. *A Preliminary Water Quality Survey of the Lower Fraser River System.* Technical Report No. 2.

Northcote, T.G. *Biology of the Lower Fraser River: A Review.* Technical Report No. 3.

Hall, K.J.; Koch, F.A.; and Yesaki, I. *Further Investigations into Water Quality Conditions in the Lower Fraser River System.* Technical Report No. 4.

Fairbairn, B. and Peterson, K. *Controlling Sawlog Debris in the Lower Fraser River.* Technical Report No. 5.

Joy, C.S. *Water Quality Models of the Lower Fraser River.* Technical Report No. 6.

Northcote, T.G.; Johnston, N.T.; and Tsumura, K. *Trace Metal Concentrations in Lower Fraser River Fishes.* Technical Report No. 7.

Northcote, T.G.; Ennis, G.L.; and Anderson, M.H. *Periphytic and Planktonic Algae of the Lower Fraser River in Relation to Water Quality Conditions.* Technical Report No. 8.

Johnston, N.T.; Albright, L.J.; Northcote, T.G.; Oloffs, P.C.; and Tsumura, K. *Chlorinated Hydrocarbon Residues in Fishes from the Lower Fraser River.* Technical Report No. 9.

Hall, K.J.; Yesaki, I.; and Chan, J. *Trace Metals and Chlorinated Hydrocarbons in the Sediments of a Metropolitan Watershed.* Technical Report No. 10.

WESTWATER BULLETIN

The Centre publishes a periodic bulletin, *Westwater,* which describes the programme of research and announces new publications. The current issue, No. 11, outlines the Centre's new major project on improving coastal resource management. Those wishing to receive *Westwater,* which is free, as well as other publications and announcements should write to Westwater Research Centre, University of British Columbia, Vancouver, V6T 1W5 or telephone 228-4956 in Vancouver.

INDEX

Achnanthes minutissima, 106
Activated carbon adsorption, 123, 127
Acute toxicity bioassay, 127
Administration:cost of, for pollution control, 148, 173, 185, 189; efficiency, 154, 169-70
Aesthetics, 164, 166-67
Agricultural producers associations, 180
Agricultural runoff: further research, 184: regulations enforcement, 180
Air stripping, 127, 134
Algae: blooms, 51, 62; pollution indicators, 106
Ammonia: need for treatment, 183; removal of, 127, 130-31
Annacis Island sewage treatment plant, 123 - 127: and Environment and Land Use Committee Secretariat, 126, 157; area served by, 123; coliform levels, 26; cost of adding to facility, 133-34; discharge volume, 37, 119; dye tracer experiments, 35
Aquatic birds, 91
Atchelitz Creek *see* Chilliwack-Atchelitz Creek

Bacterial pollution, 26, 176, 180: in Still Creek, 72
Benthic organisms, 91, 96, 105: pollution indicators, 106; pollution sensitive forms, 106-07; pollution tolerant forms, 106-07
Bioassay, 127
Biochemical oxygen demand *see* BOD
Biological activated sludge treatment, 127
Biological treatment: cost of, in fish processing, 164; effectiveness of, 132
Biomagnification, 10, 30, 45, 81, 176; in fish, 112, 127
Blood water, 167
BOD, 23: and fish processing wastes, 164; effect of nutrients on 28, effect of, on DO 36; in Chilliwack-Atchelitz Creek, 51; removal of, 37, 127, 130 - 31, 164; sources of, 176, 180; standards, 166, 180
Boundary Bay, 123
B.C. Comptroller of Water Rights, 16
B.C. Dept. of Public Works, 166
B.C. Deputy Minister of Agriculture, 16
B.C. Deputy Minister of Recreation and Travel Industry, 16
B.C. Environment and Land Use Committee Secretariat: role in use conflicts, 157; and Annacis Island sewage treatment plant, 126
B.C. Fish and Wildlife Branch: and environmental at impact assessment, 160; authority of 157; research, 169
B.C. Gazette, 16, 158
B.C. Minister of Health, 16
B.C. Packers Imperial Plant, 163-67, 173

B.C. Pollution Control Board: authority and responsibilities, 156-57; hearings, 164; objectives for industry, 158
B.C. Pollution Control Branch: and effluent standards, 160, 164; and municipal sewage treatment, 123, 126; authority and responsibilities, 156-57; proposed role in information generation and distribution, 184-85
B.C. Pollution Control Branch permits: administration of, 157, 170; and direct discharge, 163-67; and Pollution Control Act, 144; appeals, 160; application process, 16, 146, 158, 160, 163-67; enforcement of, 160, 166, inadequacies of information required for, 38, 145-46, 160, 176, 184-85 proposes improvements, 146, 184-85
B.C. Research Council, 36
B.C. Water Resources Service: monitoring activities, 187
B.C. Wildlife Federation, 145
Brunette River, 49-54:cadmium, 78; chlorinated hydrocarbon levels, 54; DDT and PCB's, 54; hydrology 68-70; land use, 68-70; lead, 79-80; toxic materials, 122, 176; trace metals, 75
Burnaby: lead from Burnaby Mountain, 80: sewage disposal, 123; toxic material in South Slope Sewer, 41
Burns Bog, 130
Burrard Inlet, 123

Cadmium: in Brunette, 78; in urban runoff, 78; levels, 32
Canada. Central Mortgage and Housing Corporation, 147
Canada. Environmental Protection Service: and cooperation with B.C. Pollution Control Branch, 160; and fish processing wastes, 164; and point sources, 169; and Pollution Control Branch permits, 16, 145, 158; and proposed pollution control agency, 171; research role, 187
Canada. Fisheries and Marine Service: and Fisheries Act, 156; and information generation, 160; and Pollution Control Branch permits, 16, 145, 158; and proposed pollution control agency, 171
Canada. Fisheries Research Board, 161, 164
Canada. Inland Waters Directorate, 187
Canada Pacific Environment Institute, 161
Canada Water Act (1970), 171
Cannery Channel, 163-67
Central Mortgage and Housing Corporation, 147
Chemical treatment, 127, 132, 134
Chilliwack sewage treatment facilities, 37
Chilliwack-Atchelitz Creek, 50: BOD, 51; DO, 51; nutrients, 51; water use, 52.